Prayer Never Fails
Especially during trials

Berney K. Dorton

Wasteland Press
www.wastelandpress.net
Shelbyville, KY USA

Prayer Never Fails:
Especially During Trials
by Berney K. Dorton

Copyright © 2011 Berney K. Dorton
ALL RIGHTS RESERVED

First Printing – April 2011
ISBN: 978-1-60047-534-4

NO PART OF THIS BOOK MAY BE REPRODUCED IN ANY FORM, BY PHOTOCOPYING OR BY ANY ELECTRONIC OR MECHANICAL MEANS, INCLUDING INFORMATION STORAGE OR RETRIEVAL SYSTEMS, WITHOUT PERMISSION IN WRITING FROM THE COPYRIGHT OWNER/AUTHOR

Printed in the U.S.A.

0 1 2 3 4 5 6 7 8 9 10 11

Dedication

To God, who inspired me to write this book. To my parents, the late Jim and Helen Whittie, who instilled in me morals and biblical principles to sustain me in life: thank you for believing in me. To my grandmother, the late Ophelia Brown, for demonstrating how to live a consecrated Christian life while remaining prayerful in a carnal world. To my devoted husband, Ronald Sr., for your love, encouragement, and support in every endeavor I pursue. To my children, whom I love: Ronald Jr, Andre, and Shannon. You are the reason why I pray. To the Good News Jail Ministry evangelism team, who possess the zeal to preach the good news to sinners. To my friends who encouraged me to use my spiritual gifts to glorify God.

All Scripture quotations, unless otherwise indicated, are taken from the Holy Bible, New International Version®. NIV® Copyright © 1973, 1978, 1984 by International Bible Society. Used by permission of Zondervan Publishing House. All rights reserved.

"Scripture taken from the New King James Version. Copyright © 1982 by Thomas Nelson, Inc. Used by permission. All rights reserved."

All of the stories in this book are true; to protect their privacy some of the names are changed.

Servant Prayer

Father God, in the name of Jesus, the crucified one, I petition You in prayer. You left us a legacy and superb example of how to pray. Prayers illustrated in the Bible were specifically for humankind. The prayers demonstrate that we must have a relationship with God, believe that  Jesus is the son of God, and pray to the Father in Jesus' name.

GOD empower us to pray with power, authority, holy boldness, and conviction. We seek You for guidance and Your will in our lives. Our endeavor is to have victorious prayer lives and anointed relationships with You. Let us feel Your presence and power in every aspect of our lives. May the Spirit of the living God endow us to be the men and women of promise that You called us to be and that we desire to become. God, you are omnipresent, omniscient, holy, infinite, and sovereign. Rest upon Your people by the power of the Holy Spirit and help us to watch and pray. Don't let us get weary in our well-doing.

Lord, our spirits are willing, but our flesh is weak. Perfect us by Your grace so we will be sufficient in our infirmities to do the will of God. Lord, allow our joy to be full. Work a miracle in our lives according to Your Divine will through the fervent prayers of the saints. We need a tsunami blessing that can only come from You. Rest, rule, and abide in us forever! Impart wisdom into our lives.

Father, bless everyone who reads this book. Enhance their prayer lives; let the power of the Holy Spirit lead them to all truth. Enable their prayer lives to be anointed and powerful beyond measure.

Father, anoint them to pray with confidence and holy boldness for themselves and others that are in need more effectively. God, You be glorified in their prayer lives. Bless their families, their marriages, and their children. Help them to stand up for the gospel and not compromise their faith. God, we are leaning and depending on You. Father, help us to walk by faith and not by sight. I give you the praise, the honor, and the glory! I thank you in advance for answering this prayer petition. In that miraculous, majestic, marvelous name of Jesus, I pray. Amen.

Table of Contents

Chapter 1
What is Prayer?   1

Chapter 2
Grandmother's Prayers   11

Chapter 3
Fervent Prayers   26

Chapter 4
The Power of Prayer   35

Chapter 5
The Storm   44

Chapter 6
Prayerfully Weathering the Storm   55

Chapter 7
Divine Intervention   63

Chapter 8
Prayerful During Death   76

Chapter 9
Intercessory Prayer   91

Chapter 10
Denied Prayer Request   114

Chapter 11
The Prayerful Church   123

Chapter 12
Spiritual Warfare 135

Chapter 13
Armor of God 147

Chapter 14
Pray and Do Not Faint 157

CHAPTER ONE

What Is Prayer?

> "Do not be anxious about anything, but in everything, by prayer and
> petition, with thanksgiving, present your requests to God.
> And the peace of God, which transcends all understanding,
> will guard your hearts and your minds in Christ Jesus."
> Philippians 4: 6–7

In life, we face a myriad of problems, which ultimately change our perspective and course of action. Sickness, death, financial hardships, and violent events expose human vulnerabilities, powerfully altering many people's lives. The imminent danger threatens our well-being and clouds our vision concerning the problem, often leaving us consumed with trepidation and perturbed about the situation.

The crises, however, are never solved by being emotionally distraught, but rather by our ability to face the situation realistically. Some people begin to question God, searching desperately for answers; others deny His divinity, while attempting to resolve pandemonium within their own power. Either way, we acquire little recourse from the utter chaos, which leaves us astonished and wondering what alternatives we possess.

Should we shake our fists in the air and shout about the unfairness of life? Should we turn to our friends for comfort or words of encouragement? On the other hand, should we cry out to God in prayer, or refrain from praying? Adversity is an equal opportunist designed to cause detriment; everyone is destined to face it, but few will overcome it.

Many people succumb to violent situations because they believe God failed to respond to their needs. In actuality, they neglected to trust God and hold on to His promises. When we exclude God from our lives, we use an intellectual approach to develop a plan for a complex problem. When our plan fails, we become dishearten and blame God for our predicament. Being autonomous is admirable in some circumstances, but when bombarded with adversities that leave us on the brink of despair, don't doubt God—trust Him! He operates in mysterious ways that are proficient in sustaining us through any trial. Regardless of the magnitude of our problems, our worries are God's concern. He functions proficiently, revealing signs, miracles, and wonders that validate His Supremacy and God's omnipotent power can't be duplicated by human intellect or strength. Prayer is the distinguishing factor that makes us realize God's grace helped us prevail through calamitous situations.

What Is Prayer?

The Greek word for prayer is *proseuche,* "a place set apart or suited for the offering of prayer."[1] "Very early in the morning, while it was still dark, Jesus got up, left the house and went off to a solitary place, where he prayed" (Mark 1:35). Jesus emphasized the significance of prayer by seeking God early in the morning. He devoted sacred time to pray in an area of seclusion, uninhibited by distractions from His disciples, Pharisees, Sadducees, and the Jewish people. As He directed His thoughts to God, Jesus sought for light in darkness, in pursuit of His destiny. He came to God with a clear conscience and a pure heart, in the hopes of strengthening His position. In return, God provided Jesus with the fortitude, perseverance, and resilience that He needed to succeed in His ministry. Jesus' unprecedented prayer life leaves a legacy for believers to adhere to and engage in when we do not have answers to our problems.

Prayer is ordained by God, honored by Christians, and relied upon when we are doubtful. Prayer permits believers to commune with God, listen to His Word, and obey His precepts. Prayer is a vital component of Christian life, just as the heart is to the body. Without the heart, blood ceases to circulate to vital organs, and death is imminent; without prayer, the spiritual growth of a Christian's life is stunted and ceases to thrive. Prayer is the heartbeat of Christianity that propels Christians to exercise their right to speak to God, meditate on His Word, and stand on His promises.

As Christians, our prayers (combined with our faith) give us a conscious sense of God's protection and provision. We overcome problems because of our prayer lives and faith in God. When our anxieties are suppressed and thanksgiving is released, God perfects our hearts and minds through prayer. Our confidence reassures us that God gives us a peace that surpasses human comprehension, regardless of any situation we may encounter.

Pray to Overcome Adversity

People who have not witnessed God's mercy may be more reluctant to pray than Christians who have experienced His grace during hardship. Many people lose hope because they do not believe

God is concerned about their situations. As a result, they grow pessimistic about their circumstances, their spiritual vision becomes obscured, and they no longer walk in faith—only agony. This visual impairment makes them incapable of visualizing a positive outcome to their problems and they become anxious and cower, and essentially retreat from praying. They then search for comfort in people, drugs, alcohol, or sexual promiscuity, which only intensifies their problems. Times like these, though tough, are not meant for abstinence from praying or for conforming to the world. Instead, cry out to God! "Lord, I need you! Come quickly! I don't know how much I can take!"

Adversity is taxing, but you do not have to fight the battle alone. If you have faith, God will assist you through unforeseen circumstances. Ecclesiastes 7:14 states, "When times are good, be happy; but when times are bad, consider: God has made the one as well as the other." We live in a toxic society and people experience seasons of prosperity and turmoil. Since God is in both situations, consider it a privilege to pray about your blessings, anguish, or despair. Express elation during times of prosperity, realizing God has blessed you. When you encounter anguish and despair, take the initiative to express your deepest emotions to God. Remember Job, a man whose life was the epitome of adversity? He profoundly teaches Christians that when we do not understand our circumstances, we need to trust God. When we encounter afflictions, we need to worship God. In times of despair, we need to pray to God. Job understood that prayer connects Divinity to humanity and sinners to a risen Savior.

Prior to an uttered word or an expressed thought, God knows the intentions of our hearts. "Prayer" permits Christian's access to an invincible God, and they are able to enter into a spiritual dimension the likes of which they have never encountered. Prayer is an indication of the spiritual condition of the soul[2]—just as breath is necessary for life, prayer is vital to the life of the soul. Through prayer, God continually nourishes our souls, because He is the Vine and we are the branches. As long as we abide in Him, we receive the nourishment that we need to flourish in spiritual maturity.

While praying, Christians receive spiritual discernment that imparts wisdom to assist them in making the correct decisions for their lives. The Holy Spirit helps Christians understand precisely what they should refrain from, as well as the thoughts and actions in which they should engage. The Holy Spirit also cautions Christians about dangerous situations and confirms their prayers. Praying permits Christians to become acquainted with God, helping them develop a fondness that grows into a strong personal relationship. This relationship is not a casual one, but rather a spiritual covenant consecrated by the Lord. As we develop a close rapport with God through prayer, we enjoy His company and He becomes a friend and companion of ours in whom we can confide and trust. As God transfuses His spiritual DNA (divinity, newness, anointing) into our souls, we become a reflection of Him and He becomes Lord of our lives, our first love, friend, and confidante.

Prayer is a dynamic expression of our faith and the gateway to praise and spiritual exhortation. Prayer is never mistaken for religious philosophy, repetitious words, or religious formality lacking in sincerity. Eloquent speech or drawn-out monologue is not a representation of honest prayer, neither is a hypocritical quest for recognition or selfish pride. Praying is a spiritual process that develops into a disciplined behavior. It is a relational experience between a spiritual Father and His children. Over time, praying becomes practical—not rehearsed, personal—not estranged.

Benefits of Prayer

Prayer is the most potent gift God has given humanity, yet many people fail to comprehend the magnitude of its power. Christians will never gain the depth or breadth of prayer until they practice what they have been taught: to pray earnestly. Our primary focus is to experience an encounter with God, who then transforms our minds to live holy and seek righteousness. This spiritual metamorphosis occurs only through prayer.

Effective prayer is productive and can be as simple as praying for God to provide a parking space, or as complex as praying for God to heal a friend from cancer. Whether we submit prayers of adoration ("Lord, I adore you"), thanksgiving ("God, I thank you for blessing me"), confession ("Lord, forgive me, for I have sinned against You"), intercession ("Lord, in the name of Jesus, please protect my family and deliver them from evil"), petition ("God, I submit this petition to you; help me become a virtuous woman with a passion to love"), or submission ("Lord, I do not know what to pray for, but help me in my darkest hour"), the type of prayer submitted should be consistent, in the full knowledge that God will supply our needs "according to His glorious riches in Christ Jesus" (Philippians 4:19).

You will reap the benefits from the seeds you have sown in prayer. "Praise the LORD, O my soul, and forget not all his benefits—who forgives all your sins and heals all your diseases, who redeems your life from the pit and crowns you with love and compassion" (Psalm 103:2–4). It is advantageous for Christians to comprehend that God is the righteous Judge who pardons our transgressions, the great Physician who heals every disease entity, and the Redeemer who purchased us with Jesus' precious blood—a sin debt that we are unable to pay. God delivered us from the pits of hell. Our human condition grieved God, and as a result, He sent Jesus to save us from perishing.

Do not forget what God has done for us, nor neglect His benefits. These spiritual benefits did not come in an employee packet, but rather as an inheritance for the believer. We are the beneficiaries to God's Kingdom; therefore, we have a right to bless the Lord as our souls rejoice. Do not slight God of your affection or be slothful to pray. As joint heirs in Christ, you are entitled to exercise your inherent rights; therefore, prevail daily in prayer as you search for God and remain patient for His answers. Continue to sow seeds of faith by praying, and the fruit of your labor will attain full fruition. As a result, your consecrated prayer life becomes strengthened and demonstrates holiness.

Prayer is the infrastructure that solidifies our faith with God's will and directives. It surpasses human limitations and reveals God's sovereignty, and its effects are powerful and efficacious. Do not forfeit your benefits by neglecting to pray or sow a seed of faith that will reap a harvest that blesses God.

Relevance of Prayer

Many people believe in prayer. Atheists deny the power of prayer, but the truth is that we all need prayer. The psalmist expounded on this concept in the lyric of a song. When you bow at the altar, please don't forget to pray for me. Whether we pray for ourselves or other people, prayer is always in order and is beneficial to everyone. David lamented, "Therefore let everyone who is godly pray to you while you may be found" (Psalm 32:6). Godly people apprehend the value and relevance of prayer; it is not on the backburner but rather in the forefront of their minds. Their conduct and dispositions display the evidence of fruitful prayer lives, and they continuously search for God.

Many people are trying to understand—with their finite minds—just how an infinite God answers prayer, but such a concept is incomprehensible. God's command is for us to trust Him with all our hearts and lean not to our own understanding; He promised that He would provide guidance in the midst of trials (see Proverbs 3:5—6). People will encounter numerous calamities, and the manner in which they handle their situations is of paramount importance. God tests our faith to determine our character and our ability to overcome trouble, and prayer links us to Him. "I have told you these things, so that in me you may have peace. In this world you will have trouble. But take heart! I have overcome the world" (John 16:33). God is not oblivious to the cries of His people; He will never abandon us. He provided deliverance for the children of Israel, and He continues to deliver people from bondage and distress today. Why? Because our cries pierce the ears of God as He listens to our petitions. External opposition caused the anguished Israelites to cry out to God, and their prayers caused Him to act against cruelty and injustice. Christians should cry out to God, praying from the perspective that God is no respecter of persons. He responded to the Israelites' cries with precision, and He will respond to yours.

God answers prayers according to His own timing. A Christian's primary objective is to submit his or her prayers in faith. Pray in Jesus' name, because His name has authoritative dominion. Trust God, believe He will respond favorably, and wait patiently without doubting. How long will we wait for our prayers to be answered? As long as it takes God to work on the problem; therefore, "We live by faith, not by sight" (2 Corinthians 5:7). We do not need a visual aid to see our destination or perceive where God is taking us. Faith is the guiding principle we adhere to in order to solve our problems, and our faith is in God, who is the compass of our lives. Faith provides the means for us to face our trials with courage. In spite of the turmoil surrounding us, we possess bravery to overcome situations, and our courage enables us to take action; we are the victors, not the victims.

Prayer is the predominant factor that prevents us from faltering. When you find yourself vacillating under the pressures of life, do not hesitate to pray; those valley experiences will be your most momentous ones, because God is refining you throughout the entire ordeal in order to help develop your spiritual maturity. Ultimately, your experience will enhance your faith and you will serve as a testimony to others. Every force attempting to destroy you will be incapable of accomplishing its mission. When God steps in, every bleak situation turns into a ray of hope.

What should you do in the face of adversity? Should you shy away from the problem and curl up into the fetal position? Heaven forbid! Absolutely not! Enduring adversity is difficult, but it becomes more complex without God. Entreat God in prayer, and pray until you receive the victory! Press your way from the valley to the mountaintop; your valley experiences lead to mountaintop victories. Press your way through pain, agony, disappointment, sickness, doubt, and fear. God is calling you to a higher standard through the testing of your faith. Yes, it will be painful and uncomfortable. Yes, you may experience times when you want to surrender—but remember, if you do not face the challenge, you will definitely experience defeat.

"God is our refuge and strength, an ever-present help in trouble" (Psalm 46:1). No one finds pleasure in enduring trials, but we gain an invaluable foretaste of God's blessings. By virtue of His nature, He will accomplish His will and purpose for our lives despite the trials we encounter. In times of adversity remember God's Word; it will not return void. We should not be fearful of what lies ahead. Instead, draw on the Holy Spirit that God has endowed within you, trust God as you put your faith into action, and entreat God with "specific prayers." His divinity, newness, and anointing will enable you to endure hardship. Think positively and speak to your situation: "My faith is greater than my circumstance."

CHAPTER TWO

Grandmother's Prayers

"And lead us not into temptation, but deliver us from the evil one."
Matthew 6:13

I've always believed that our grandparents have our best interests at heart. They warn us to avoid engaging in evil deeds and to refuse to allow detriment to enter into our lives. My grandmother, Ophelia, was a devout Christian who believed in prayer. She prayed consistently for God to deliver us from sin and evil. She never scolded us about our carnal behavior—instead, she prayed. She read the Bible faithfully and incorporated biblical principles into her life. She carried her Bible with her everywhere she traveled; it was her companion, and she never left home without it. Her godly character demonstrated her sincerity about her salvation to others. People loved and respected my grandmother; they often requested prayer from her, and she cheerfully consented.

Grandmother would send prayer cloths to her grandchildren from Beaumont, Texas, to California, for us to pin to our pajamas. As a child, I often looked forward to receiving the prayer cloth. Until now, I never realized the magnitude of her prayer life. Both the time she spent making the prayer cloths and the prayers that she prayed influenced my life tremendously. The prayer cloths were symbolic of a shield of protection to keep us out of harm's way, and her consecrated prayer life identified her love for God and intimacy, as well as her concerns and love for her grandchildren.

I thank God for my grandmother's passion to pray. She was a prayer warrior who spent ample time with God, and she never wavered in her faith. When she died, several people asked our family for her Bible, but we denied their request. We decided to bury her with her sword, because they were inseparable. Her epitaph read, "I have fought the good fight, I have finished the race, I have kept the faith" (2 Timothy 4:7). She fought an impeccable race for us when we could not fight spiritually for ourselves. She knew evil forces could destroy us; nevertheless, she prevailed in prayer, exhibiting a hedge of protection and a spiritual fortress of power. She sowed a seed of faith in good soil, which matured to embrace the spirit of prayer. When I was unable to pray for myself, my grandmother prayed for me. I have gleaned two significant biblical principles from my grandmother's life: (1) love the Lord with all my heart, mind, and soul; and (2) a wholesome prayer life exhibits a godly life, which allows people to see the light of Christ residing in you. For this reason, I emphasize five reasons to pray.

Five Reasons for Prayer

Prayer is a lifestyle, not a rudimentary chore. Because prayer is the underpinning of Christians' faith, we must engage in prayer wholeheartedly.

1. *Pray to confess and confront the sin in our lives.* What makes a husband viciously shoot and stab his wife, slit his children's throats, and set their home on fire to conceal the evidence? Why do sons

murder their parents with blunt objects without exhibiting any signs of remorse? Why would a deranged mother hurl her three children off a bridge? How can men go on a ballistic rampage and viciously murder their coworkers, then shoot themselves? Why do sexual predators maliciously rape and molest innocent children, tossing their remains in the sea or stuffing their remains in suitcases? How can terrorists strap themselves to bombs, killing innocent people? Why do some preachers solicit prostitutes for rendezvous and use illegal drugs?

Sin! Sin is evil, contagious, and deadly. The entrance of sin is the pathway to evil. Sin infiltrates our lives, distorts our perspectives, and leaves us disillusioned about God's judgment. Galatians 3:22 proclaims, "But the Scripture declares that the whole world is a prisoner of sin." Because of sin, we "all fall short of the glory of God" (Romans 3:23). God cannot reveal His glory to sinners. God hates sin! He is sinless, and man is sinful. God cannot embrace man's sinful nature; rather, He retreats from it. God is unwilling to communicate with unholy people who are unclean vessels filled with filth and decay. He requires a spiritual transformation, which operates within a man's heart, and this experience occurs only through repentance and prayer. When sin is exposed, lives are changed, and repenting hearts restrain us from repeating the offenses. As a result, our personal relationships with Christ are saved, and not severed.

David exclaimed, "Surely I was sinful at birth, sinful from the time my mother conceived me" (Psalm 51:5). The Apostle Paul extrapolates that "sin nature is always present, even when he desires to make the correct decision: evil is at hand. Your adversary is working against you. Then he realizes it is not him, but the sin that resides within him warring against his mind" (Romans 7:17). This dilemma originates from a confrontation between the flesh and the Holy Spirit. Flesh is the embodiment of sin that must be under the submission of the Holy Spirit. When the flesh overrides the Holy Spirit, an unnerving situation evolves. The Holy Spirit is grieved. Offending the Holy Spirit is equally offensive to God, causing Him great anguish and pain—because His Spirit is sealed within us as a mark of inheritance and ownership. The Holy Spirit is an intelligent person who is personally involved in our lives to reveal invaluable truth. Once grieved, the Holy Spirit is unable to operate efficiently according to God's will.

Your resentment and rebellious conduct causes you to return to past behaviors that God has redeemed you from; this repulsive attitude immensely insults the Holy Spirit and God. As a result, ungodly behavior is exhibited as sin captivates our thoughts and lures us into ungodly predicaments. For example: "I knew he was married, but I dated him because he told me he is divorcing his wife," or "I stole the dress because I did not have the money to pay for it," or "I lied because I thought I could get away with it." Sin is powerful, and it can wreck our lives when we submit to its powerful lure. Sins concealed from the human eye are still visible to God. Many people alienate themselves from God because their lives reflect carnal appetites; they live contrary to godly principles. But there is no prosperity in sin—only judgment

Prayer gives us the power to overcome our sinful behavior and have victory over our evil deeds, as it transforms' our minds. We are more conscientious of our actions and our lives portray an immeasurable sense of accountability, which in essence reflects a positive change that occurred from within. Prudent decisions are made concerning our lives because of prayer, and the Holy Spirit is our guidance counselor who steers us in the right direction.

"Confession" is derived from the Greek work *homologeo*, meaning "to say the same thing, to agree, concur."[3] God appreciates honesty and He acknowledges the confession of our sins, which is crucial in maintaining a relationship with Him. For Christians, confession is not an option; it is an obligation to Christ that helps us recognize our carnality. "He who conceals his sins does not prosper, but whoever confesses and renounces them finds mercy" (Proverbs 28:13). We are aware of God's character and are unworthy of His mercy, but He extends mercy to those who renounce sin. A guilty conscience is relieved by confession of sins, conveying to God that we are remorseful for our thoughts and actions that led to undesirable conduct. Abandoning contentious behavior allows us to receive God's mercy instead of His punishment. Confession is good for the soul, and it reunites us with Christ. By praying, condemnation is withheld and God's forgiveness is granted. Prayer reinforces our obligation to live prosperous lives without guilt. We can declare, "Blessed is the man whose sin the LORD does not count against him and in whose spirit is no deceit" (Psalm 32:2).

2. *Pray to thank God for His blessings.* The Bible says, "Pray continually; give thanks in all circumstances, for this is God's will for you in Christ Jesus" (1Thessalonians 5:17—18). Christians pray; sinners don't. People who trust God understand that *prayerfulness*

draws you closer to God and *prayerlessness* turns you away. Prayer should be our initial response instead of our last-ditch effort. Every aspect of our lives requires prayer, and praying faithfully receives God's attention. Prayer is not contingent upon our capabilities, but rather on God's accountability.

Glean from these examples of people who sincerely prayed:

- Jesus conscientiously prayed throughout His life. He sought solitude and received gratification from God. He prayed on the mountaintop, in the synagogue, in people's homes, and for His disciples (Matthew 5:1, Luke 4:1, 16, Mark 1:35, John 17:9).
- Daniel prayed faithfully three times a day, denouncing pagan beliefs while he was a captive in Babylon (Daniel 6:10).
- The Apostle Paul never ceased to pray while he was fastened in stocks and chains (Acts 16:24).
- Elisha prayed for a double portion of Elijah's spirit, and it was granted to him (2 Kings 2:9).
- Shadrach, Meshach, and Abednego prayed in the fiery furnace and were delivered unharmed from the intensity of the heat (Daniel 3:19).
- Elisha prayed for God to blind the Aramean army, and blindness engulfed their eyes (2 Kings 6:18).
- Hezekiah's tearful prayer vindicated him from his death sentence, and a merciful God added fifteen years to his life (2 Kings 20:1, 6).

These patriarchs understood God's attributes and His character. They understood that God is consistent when they are inconsistent, sovereign when they are inferior, and powerful when they are powerless. From their experiences, they began to thank God. They were mindful of the blessings that God had promised and delivered to them, and as they thanked God, they began to praise Him. Thankfulness demonstrates our appreciation for God's loving kindness. We are rejoicing instead of complaining about our problems, and our focus is on God—not the situation.

Thanksgiving and prayer work simultaneously to attain spiritual bliss. "Give thanks to the LORD, for he is good; his love endures forever" (Psalm 107:1). This declaration encourages people to give thanks unto the Lord because they have experienced God's love, His goodness, His Divine intervention, and witnessed their situations change favorably. They have seen the keen aspect of God's capability to change erroneous behavior and situations as He instills wisdom into our consciences, skillfully cultivating His Word. Perverted minds change, as well as people's hearts and lifestyles. While praying, thank God for His spiritual influence and the specific blessings that you have received. God's mercy is new every morning, and He cares for our welfare. Personally thank God for His blessings, provision, and generosity and remind Him of your gratitude.

I thank God for mercy, which has brought me through extreme circumstances. Mercy kept me from being devastated and allowed me to be strong at my weakest moment. "Enter his gates with thanksgiving and his courts with praise; give thanks to him and praise his name" (Psalm 100:4). I thank God for being able to enter into His gates with spontaneous praise. I thank God for my health and strength. I thank God for my sanity. I thank God for the power of the Holy Spirit that reveals truth. I thank God for my family, friends, and enemies. I thank God for the trials that help build my Christian character and conduct. Ultimately, I thank God for Jesus and the Holy Spirit within me. I thank God for the atoning blood of Jesus and for receiving salvation and eternal life.

God has entrusted humanity with the best gift man has ever received: Jesus Christ. Christians are peculiar people—a royal priesthood; as such, thankfulness should resonate within our spirits consistently. The prayer lives of Christians should automatically include thanks on a consistent basis. Thankfulness arises when we reflect on situations that changed because of God's intervention. Reflect on the signs, miracles, and wonders that God has personally performed in your life, and thank Him because those precious moments helped you to realize His goodness. Never forget to thank God for everything; He is Lord of our lives and the keeper of our souls.

3. *Pray to develop intimacy with God.* James 4:8 accentuates this point: "Come near to God and he will come near to you. Wash your hands, you sinners, and purify your hearts, you double-minded." God is not intimate with everyone; therefore, everyone cannot be intimate with God. He does not indulge in erotic pleasures or sexual fantasies as humans do. Pornography is taboo to God. He is Holy. He created man, and man does not entice Him with acts of lewdness. He draws near to people who possess sincerity of heart, godly characteristics, and prudent behavior.

Who can enter into the presence of God? Who can worship a holy God? Who can develop an intimate relationship with God? It is the people who possess clean hands and pure hearts, and people who abstain from debasing their morals. They present themselves upright before the Lord in their deeds and actions, and they perform good works in spite of evil circumstances. In God's presence, their conduct is prudent—not tainted—and they participate in evangelism instead of criticism, while refraining from evil works and carnal pleasures.

God yearns for intimacy, and He seeks people who are transparent and truthful and who display godly conduct; these individuals can enter into His presence because of their faith. Godly people desire more of God's presence and wisdom and less of their fleshly desires. They refrain from cursing, drunkenness, indulging in adultery, fornication or participating in criticizing or ridiculing people who are less fortunate then they are. They seek after the kingdom of God and His righteousness; yearning for an intimate relationship. Once developed, an astonishing transformation occurs: people become transparent, and every sin is revealed, every thought heard, every evil deed exposed. Intimacy, allows us to disclose personal information we would be reluctant to divulge to others.

God is a Spirit, and the Holy Spirit that dwells richly within our hearts enables us to communicate spiritually with Him. Because of this robust relationship, God releases His wisdom, will, precepts, and secrets. Prayer prepares our hearts and minds to be submissive to God's instruction and receptive to His chastening.

Prayer is the fundamental framework that permits intimacy to develop, and this spiritual relationship requires commitment and discipline. This intimate relationship develops through reading the Bible, meditation, prayer, and fasting. Privately praying engages the individual's attention and focus on God. This spiritual relationship reveals God's holiness and transforms our carnal minds, and the transformation permits us to love God as He ministers to our mortal souls. God's attributes become apparent to us, and we acknowledge that He is infinite, without limitation or boundaries. Omnipotent, God is powerful beyond measure. Omnipresent, He is everywhere at the same time. Omniscient, He is knowledgeable about everything. God is holy; He reveals His purity and righteousness continually in our lives.

How can we approach a holy God? What does it take to draw closer to Him? It requires a willing spirit that will reverence Him, worship Him, love Him, praise Him, and keep His commandments. When we turn our souls to God, He turns His heart toward us. He bestows blessings upon His people, which is the ultimate reward of an intimate relationship. This conscious decision is fostered by a desire to know God personally. God yearns for intimacy, and we should yearn to be intimate with God. Pray affectionately and sincerely to attain a robust relationship with Him.

4. *Pray for cleansing and restoration.* Sin contaminates us; Jesus' atoning blood cleanses us. Confession of sins receives God's forgiveness and attention. David pleaded with God to "cleanse me with hyssop, and I will be clean; wash me, and I will be whiter than snow" (Psalm 51:7). Spiritual cleansing is imperative to receiving the blessing of God. To "cleanse" means to remove the substance that caused us to become unrighteous, defiled, and contaminated. The old

proverb, "Cleanliness is next to godliness" is true; God cleanses us from all impurities, enabling us to be as refined as pure gold.

When you sin against God, repentance is of the upmost importance. Acknowledge your faults, ask God for forgiveness, and He will cleanse you from all unrighteous conduct, thoughts, desires, and actions. Acknowledging sin illustrates a desire to change your behavior, and repentance illustrates a sincere change in your attitude, thoughts, and mind, turning you away from sin towards God. When you are conscious of your ability to sin you are more inclined to listen to the prompting of the Holy Spirit and refrain from exhibiting past behaviors.

David was remorseful for his sinful actions and he repented and pleaded for forgiveness. He jeopardized and dishonored his relationship with God because of his adulterous affair with Bathsheba; David petitioned God in prayer not to take His spirit away from him but to restore his joy. When there is no joy, there is no peace, and despair enters into our lives. "The joy of the Lord is your strength" (Nehemiah 8:10). Without strength, we do not possess power. Without joy, weakness transcends. Because of his guilty conscience, David could not rejoice in the Lord. "Joy" means "the emotion of great delight or happiness caused by something exceptionally good or satisfying; keen pleasure; elation."[4] "Strength" is inherent capacity to manifest energy, to endure, and to resist."[5] David's ability to resist stress and his power to resist temptation were weak. Vulnerable David prayed sincerely because he lacked the potential to stand, overcome, and resist compromising predicaments that caused him to sin. From this biblical illustration, we can conclude that sin separates us from God and that we lose the ability to joyfully engage in praise and worship. 1 John 1:8—9 declares, "If we claim to be without sin, we deceive ourselves and the truth is not in us. If we confess our sins, he is faithful and just and will forgive us our sins and purify us from all unrighteousness." Righteousness emerges from God; unrighteousness comes from sin. God knows we are sinners, but we deny that we have sinned. This makes us liars in God's presence, which is one of the most seven deadliest sins. Satan is the father of lies, and lies associate us with him; therefore, we are guilty by association. Deception is a characteristic of Satan, which essentially distorts our perception of truth. God is willing to forgive, but only if we do not forget that we have sinned against Him. Therefore, pray truthfully while addressing your problems to increase your faith and affirm God's promises. We are strongest against sin when we are on our knees, praying while avoiding compromising situations. Pray for restoration to return to your original state of holiness.

Spiritual restoration occurs when fleshly desires are denied. Restoration provides God the opportunity to prevent a downward spiral of spiritual decay. Humble yourself before the Lord. Where there is brokenness, allow the Lord to restore your relationship with Him. This spiritual restoration occurs from praying and seeking God for instructions. God reestablishes us through our faith and prayer. His intention is for our hearts, souls, and minds to love Him, trust Him, and obey Him. His desire is to restore us to states of godliness while changing imperfections within us—despite our rebellious attitudes, ungrateful hearts, and insecurities. Restoration occurs because of God's faithfulness, not our hopelessness. Cleansing and restoration are the essential components that sustain our relationships with God; thus, it is of paramount importance to pray and ask God for forgiveness every time we sin. Prayer keeps us on God's mind as He forgives, cleanses, and restores our souls. We can then proclaim, "Bless the LORD, O my soul; And all that is within me, bless His holy name" (Psalm 103:1 NKJV).

5. *The righteous prayers availeth much.* Righteous people seek God, and unrighteous people seek selfish gain. "The eyes of the LORD are on the righteous, and his ears are attentive to their cry" (Psalm 34:15). God listens to righteous prayers: "And if we are careful to obey all this law before the LORD our God, as he has commanded us, that will be our righteousness" (Deuteronomy 6:25). What constitutes righteousness? Righteousness is exhibited in men and women who are morally upright and possess integrity and self-control. They live in accordance to God's Word and obey His commandments, performing the right actions with the right attitudes. Righteous people listen attentively when God speaks, as they follow the directives of the Holy Spirit. Their obedience signifies their adoration, reverence, and love for God. They apprehend clearly "what the righteous desire will be granted" (Proverbs 10:24). God delights in hearing and receiving prayers from people who display sincerity about their prayer lives. Their request will be granted.

"Avail" means, "to be of use or value to; profit; advantage." The righteous prayers are valuable, effective, and powerful; they do not possess monetary value, but spiritual merit. "Availeth much" signifies that our prayers are great in quantity, measure, or degree.[6] Righteous people are compelled to pray with vigor, demonstrating a spiritual tenacity that takes captive every demonic thought or plot. *Dunamis* prayers tear down demonic forces of evil in the heavenly realms. "*Dunamis*" means "power, or force."

The Holy Spirit intercedes with utterance, making our prayers congruent with God's will, and the Holy Spirit removes all selfishness, doubt, and worry as it searches the mind of God and seizes the opportunity to uphold saints in prayer. The righteous pray with assurance and confidence, believing God will make provision for our necessities, though at times, we become disheartened and it feels like we are being torn down. We can pray in the still of the night or in the day because God never slumbers or sleeps. We cannot neglect prayer because it is our lifeline to God. His power has dominion over every opposition in our lives, and He blesses us instead of condemning us for our disobedience.

The righteous pray while consciously seeking God for answers and reassurance, and the spirit of faith permits us to stand on God's Word and receive His promises. We cast our cares on Him because He is capable of carrying our burdens, and as we pray to Him, we receive forgiveness, instructions, mercy, and grace. What He does in the spiritual realm is tangible evidence exhibited in our lives. What we hope for in faith becomes apparent from the fruition of our prayers.

Staying prayerful invigorates us for the next battle. We begin to develop spiritual maturity in our Christian walk. We are no longer babes in Christ, but we become good and faithful servants of the Lord. We have become beacons of light in a dark world, and we have attained the status of seasoned Christians who possess salt that has not lost its flavor.

Our hope is in Jesus Christ and His righteousness. This living hope keeps us prayerful as we discover consolation and answers to our prayers. Prayer strengthens our relationship with God and gives us guidance, spiritual blessings, renewed hope, and insurmountable faith.

Righteous men pray; ungodly men stray away from God. Remember, none but the righteous shall see God. "I was young and now I am old, yet I have never seen the righteous forsaken or their children begging bread" (Psalm 37:25). Righteous prayers avail because of godly behavior and commitment to God through the guidance of the Holy Spirit.

Numerous reasons exist to pray, but we must understand the magnitude of prayer's power. Execute a plan to incorporate a daily regimen to pray. Whether you pray to confess your sins, utter thankfulness, develop intimacy with God, or for restoration or spiritual cleansing, implement prayer into your daily life. Jesus left us specific instructions about prayer: honor God by remaining prayerful, and do not neglect to use the power God has given you, teach your children and grandchildren to pray, and live the life you earnestly pray about.

CHAPTER THREE

Fervent Prayers

*"In the morning, O LORD, you hear my voice;
in the morning I lay my requests before you and wait in expectation."*
Psalm 5:3

The phone rang at 5:00 a.m. Although I was sleepy, I struggled to wake up to answer it. I heard my prayer partner's voice. Karen said, "Wake up, prayer partner! It's prayer time!"

I responded, "Praise the Lord!" and we began to pray. We have touched and agreed at the throne of grace for over ten years, consistently praying for our churches, families, pastors, community, youth, nation, and friends. We made a commitment to pray daily because we believe in the power of prayer. We have witnessed the hand of God move in our lives miraculously, transforming chaotic situations into peaceful ones. Through prayer, our faith and trust in God has increased, and we have become stronger in the Lord and his mighty power (Ephesians 6:10).

This particular morning, Karen sounded troubled as we interceded in prayer. As she proceeded to pray she began to cry, and I discerned that she was discouraged. I listened attentively as she continued to pray fervently. As she poured out her soul to God, I could feel her agony. Karen is a virtuous woman and a relentless prayer warrior who loves the Lord, so I prayed silently within my heart that God would prevail in her situation. When we finished praying, I decided to arrange for a prayer meeting at my home. I discussed my concerns with Karen, and she agreed with my decision.

The Book of Acts, Chapter 12, displays vivid illustrations of a prayer meeting held at the home of Mary, the mother of Mark. The great persecution and Peter's arrest caused an emergent need for the church to pray zealously, so the saints assembled a prayer vigil to intercede for Peter to prevent his execution. While they remained engrosssed in prayer, Peter knocked on the gate. Unbeknownst to them, their prayers were answered. Solidarity in prayer brings blessings from God, and my prayer is for the same harmonious spirit to reside in my home.

Prayer Meeting

"Many women do noble things, but you surpass them all. Charm is deceptive, and beauty is fleeting; but a woman who fears the Lord is to be praised" (Proverbs 31:29—30). For several years, I have invited anointed women of God to my home to pray. These God-fearing women are diligent prayer warriors; they have witnessed the power of God transcend through the Holy Spirit on their behalf, they call on Jesus and praise His name, and they are confident God will miraculously respond and come to their aid.

I have known some of these women since childhood; others, I met through mutual acquaintances. Some are ministers, evangelists, and missionaries who love God. He has blessed our friendships to coincide for a reason and a season, and I am grateful that He ordained this to happen, because these women are precious jewels and very dear to me.

When I invite them to pray, their initial responses are always spontaneous and positive. I phone them and simply say, "It's prayer time!" and they respond with, "I'm ready!" or "Prayer is needed," or "I'm going through." Have you scheduled a date for the prayer meeting?

I provide them with the information, and then I request them to do three things prior to the prayer meeting: (1) pray until they arrive at my home, (2) bring their Bibles, and (3) bring their favorite dish for fellowship. When they arrive at my home, we embrace one another in sisterly love, and I feel God's power. Although we are from different churches and ethnic backgrounds, we represent the Body of Christ, and we are like-minded and on one accord in prayer. These zealous, God fearing women are serious about their prayer lives; they have witnessed the positive results of answered prayers. We have the same spiritual mentality as the parishioners in Acts: to pray, wait, and expect a miracle. Their insurmountable faith positions them to prevail in prayer, without doubting God's capabilities. They know God, and God knows them. He grants us the desires of our hearts when we delight ourselves in Him.

God has given us power to execute against the throne of Satan, which we do by trampling on snakes, scorpions, and all the power of the enemy (Luke 10:19). Our enemy is incapable of harming us because we possess the resurrection power of God. We tear down strongholds when we pray and lay prostrate on our prayer cloths. We read scriptures, sing hymns, and testify about the goodness of the Lord. The Bible declares, "They overcame him (Satan) by the blood of the Lamb and by the word of their testimony" (Revelation 12:11).

Our testimonies expose our sins and prevent Satan from accusing us of disorderly conduct and disobedience towards God. While we are praying in the spirit, we seek the Lord and ask for guidance in our lives while thanking God for His provision. We empty out these earthen vessels and allow God to fill us with fire!

"Many are the afflictions of the righteous, But the LORD delivers him out of them all" (Psalm 34:19 NKJV). We would not have a praise report if we did not endure afflictions. Many of us have endured trials while God has tested our faith and given us grace. He's heard our pleas and given us mercy. He healed one of the women from cancer, and now she is in remission. He breathed the breath of life into the body of one of our sisters who was on life support. God comforted me during the death of my mother and father and He healed my body, allowing me to recuperate from surgery without pain. He opened up the door for my television ministry while uniting my family. God has given us different ministries and counseled several women during their marital separations.

Through all of these tribulations, we remained prayerful and continued to speak at church engagements, attend intercessory prayer meetings, sing in the choir, and minister to inmates in jail—all of which has allowed us to spread the gospel to lost souls. We are salt, and we refuse to lose our flavor. All honor and glory belongs to Him. We exhort God and magnify His name! God is glorified in our praise for renewing our spiritual walk with Him. These trials have drawn us closer to God, and the tests have transformed into testimonies.

These daughters of Zion are aware of their responsibilities to pray sincerely with heartfelt prayers for themselves and others. They believe "the effective, fervent prayer of a righteous man avails much" (James 5:16 NKJV). *Effectual* prayers produce the effect desired or intended, having adequate power or force to produce the effect.[7] *Fervent* prayers are ardent; they are hot, a burning desire of the saint, having or illustrating great warmth or intensity and earnest [ness]."[8]

We possess a burning passion to advance the kingdom of God; our intentions are to be transparent before Him, possessing a spirit of humility and sincerity. Our prayers are like hot coals burning with intensity and power—they produce a potent effect that causes God to bless His Word. God attentively listens to the righteous. "Therefore, I tell you, whatever you ask for in prayer, believe that you have received it, and it will be yours" (Mark 11:24).

Paul and Silas' Powerful Prayers

Paul and Silas were men of insurmountable faith who were familiar with the power of prayer. They were in a gruesome situation: attacked by a vicious crowd, beaten with rods, falsely accused, and stripped of their dignity, and their feet were fastened in stocks (Acts 16:22). Their incarceration did not inhibit them from praying at midnight. Paul and Silas prayed in the maximum-security section of the prison; they were not intimidated by the guards or their surroundings. Despite their dismal predicament, Paul and Silas began to sing and pray as the prisoners listened attentively (Acts 16:25). The prisoners and the guards were both their captive audience and their parishioners. Can you hear them singing, "Amazing grace, how sweet the sound that saved a wretch like me. I once was lost, but now I'm found, was blind, but know I see?" Perhaps they might have sung,

"Oh, how I love Jesus because He first loved me," or "How great Thou art."

Then they began to have devotion, praying to God and saying, "God, we love you; God, we extol you, and we magnify Your holy name. You are God, and there is no God like Jehovah. You are King of Kings, and Lord of Lords. We worship and adore You in the beauty of Your holiness. We give You praise, honor, and glory, because of who You are. You are faithful and trustworthy, omnipotent, omniscient, infinite, self-existing. Oh God, you allowed us to see a new dawning, and we thank You for delivering us from our enemies' hands. Bless those who hear and prepare their hearts and minds to receive the infallible truth, which comes from an irrefutable God. Touch the prisoners' hearts, Heavenly Father, right now! Touch them, Lord Jesus, with Your omnipotent power and love! Touch them, Lord, and redeem them from the pits of hell! Consecrate their hearts and minds to receive You. Let them worship the true and living God. Cover them right now, Father, in the blood of the crucified Lamb. The blood will never lose its power; it replenishes us daily. Now, Everlasting King, You be glorified in this jail, amen." Salvation is found in no one else, for there is no other name under heaven given to men by which we must be saved" (Acts 4:12).

God was in the midst of Paul and Silas' prayers. According to Acts 16: 26-28, the earth began to vibrate, and a violent earthquake happened. The foundation of the prison was shaken, and all the prisoners' doors flew open. Every prisoner's chain came loose, but the prisoners did not escape. They were astonished by the prayer and confounded by the earthquake as God opened their ears to hear

Spiritual revelation; they were under arrest by the Holy Spirit, and God was moving in their presence. When true praise, worship, and adoration are rendered unto Almighty God, supernatural events occur, and God's *Shekinah* glory appears. *Shekinah* means the presence of God on earth or a symbol or manifestation of His presence.[9] God inhabits the praises of His people, and when praises are expressed, blessings are released. God revealed to Paul and Silas the magnitude of His power, and as a result, people were released from bondage as God annihilated physical and mental shackles of unbelief. Paul and Silas preached salvation, and their ardent prayers blessed the jailer and the prisoners; as a result, the jailer's entire household was saved.

Prayer is powerful and has the potential to convict people of their sins and open their hearts to receive salvation. Prayer is often accompanied by praise and springs forth as a testament to God's mercy and loving kindness. Paul's and Silas "praise" demonstrate an explicit expression of adoration for God and reverence for His authority, and their jovial singing represents grateful hearts that trust and depend on Him. God adores praise and He's delighted when we sing, dance, and shout with triumphant voices. Regardless of your circumstances, remain prayerful and praise God, because prayer and praise has a momentous effect on His reactions and your outcome.

"Consequently, faith comes from hearing the message, and the message is heard through the word of Christ" (Romans 10:17). All saints are responsible for the measure of faith God has given us (Romans 12:3). Saints who operate in the measure of faith complement one another and are like-minded, united, and vigilant in prayer. Paul and Silas' bodacious prayers exhibited their faith during hardships, and their good works are admirable characteristics in the sight of the Lord. Because of their prayers, commitment, and adoration for God, they won souls for God's kingdom.

We must ask ourselves this question: In the midst of trials and tribulations, do we believe that God will sustain us and answer our prayers in spite of the turmoil and confusion? Can we witness to people effectively when we are enduring suffering? Remember, God's eye is on the righteous, and His ear is attentive to our prayers. We have access to God twenty-four hours a day, seven days a week, three hundred and sixty-five days of the year. Praise Him in the midst of your trials, and He will hear your cry and respond to your needs.

Prayer of Faith

Lord Jesus, prevent us from buckling under pressure. Lord, Your yoke is easy, and Your burdens are light; therefore, we cast our cares on You. We cast every emotion, doubt, and fear that will inhibit us from trusting You and giving You praise. The Word of God beckons us to, "Come to me, all you who are weary and burdened, and I will give you rest" (Matthew 11:28). We come in humility, transparent and honest. Father, because of our problems, disappointments, and mishaps, do not let our hearts be troubled. Break the chains of bondage, fear, and intimidation. Help us to prevail through the valley experiences in our lives, and give us the tenacity to press forward through every obstacle and opposition. We know that trials come to tests our faith, so increase our faith to the fullest measure. Let us be able to have a good report like Paul and Silas. Let our faith be a testament to our triumph over discouragement and despair. Let us never lose hope, and let us pray until the outcome changes. While we are in transition, assist us to pray fervently and with incredible zeal that enables us to praise you in spite of our circumstances. Invigorate us to proclaim the gospel story about God's goodness and His mercy, in Jesus name, amen.

CHAPTER FOUR

The Power of Prayer

> "I cried out to him with my mouth; his praise was on my tongue. If I had cherished sin in my heart, the Lord would not have listened, but God has surely listened and heard my voice in prayer. Praise be to God, who has not rejected my prayer or withheld his love from me!"
> Psalm 66:17–20

It was midnight when the phone rang; reluctantly, I answered it.

She said, "Berney, Brian has been shot! Meet us at the hospital!"

I hung up the phone, shook my husband, and told him to wake up. "Ronald, Rita said Brian has been shot! Get dressed—we have to go to the hospital!" (Rita is Ronald's sister and Brian's mother.)

He responded, "What?"

I repeated what his sister had told me. The commotion woke up the entire household; our children were in shock after they overheard the devastating news.

They asked me, "What happened?"

I said, "I don't know, but we need to get to the hospital right away."

As we drove to the hospital, there was complete silence in the car. I thought, *Why would anyone want to shoot Brian?* Brian was our nephew. He was 21 years old and a handsome, adorable young man with hazel eyes and a radiant smile. When we arrived at the emergency entrance of the hospital, we saw numerous young people crying and embracing one another. As we exited the car, I saw our niece,

Ashley (Brian's younger sister); she was distraught and crying uncontrollably.

I walked up to her and asked, "What happened?"

She exclaimed, "I don't know—they just shot him!" And she continued to cry.

I asked, "Where is your mother?"

Ashley replied, "In the emergency room."

Later that evening, we learned that Brian had been the victim of a drive-by shooting. Brian and Rita, his mother, had spent the evening celebrating his girlfriend's mother's birthday at a church event. After the party, Brian and Rita went to visit a close friend nearby. He was sitting in his car, waiting for one of his friends to arrive to meet him when the neighbors heard a series of gunshots. When they went to investigate the commotion, they discovered Brian bleeding profusely inside his car. Someone called the emergency medical team, and Brian was transferred to the hospital. The medical personnel worked on him nonstop while they were in transit.

We met Rita inside the emergency room. As we affectionately embraced, I asked if Brian was conscious.

She replied, "I don't know. I saw the paramedics trying to revive him while they were transporting him to the hospital."

We waited patiently—seemingly for hours—then we asked the emergency nurse the status of Brian Lester. She said the physician was working on him and that she would return later to update the family about his condition. Finally, the physician on duty asked for the family to gather in the chapel. When she entered the room, she asked, "Who is the mother of the patient?"

Rita responded, "I am."

The physician said, "Brian sustained severe gunshot wounds, and they exhausted every possibility to save his life." Then she said, "He expired."

Before she completed the sentence, Brian's sister, Ashley, sprinted out of the room, crying, and shouted, "Oh, no, no, no, no!"

Sorrow and grief engulfed the room, and my children began to cry.

My husband said, "Rita, I'm sorry."

I shook my head and said, "What a senseless death."

We were all in shock, but Rita was calm as she picked up the phone. She said, "I have to contact his father." She was very composed. God comforted her during the unseemly nightmare as He embraced her with peace that surpasses all understanding.

I spoke with the physician privately while Rita was on the phone and asked her if his mother could view Brian's body. Later, I asked Rita if she wanted to view it.

She said, "Yes."

I said, "Are you sure?"

She said, "Yes."

I told her I would go into the room with her.

As we proceeded into the room, a police officer intervened and informed us that we could not view Brian's body because they were collecting forensic evidence for the case.

With a soft, tranquil voice and humble spirit, Rita looked directly into the officer's eyes and said, "I want to see my son; I will not touch him."

The officer agreed to let her enter the room, and my husband and I accompanied her. I didn't know how she would react, but we were there for moral support.

We entered the room together, and Rita gazed at Brian's lifeless body as it lay against the stark white sheets. She did not cry out or show any emotion; she just looked at him with sympathetic eyes and shook her head. We were grief-stricken as we gazed at Brian's remains; it is terrifying to witness a mother identify her son's body after such a heartless crime.

When we left the emergency room, numerous young people were outside crying, devastated by the news.

Rita hugged me with a vice-like grip and whispered in my ear, "Berney, pray for me."

I assured her that I would. I also asked the church to pray for her and our family. God heard Rita's prayer request and our petition. I witnessed God move expeditiously with an abundance of love. People came from Louisiana, Los Angeles, San Francisco, and Oakland, California, to give their condolences, sincere prayers, and love. Brian's death deeply grieved our family and his friends, but his life positively influenced people who he was acquainted with. His friends cried and embraced one another at the funeral, and we felt their pain. At the gravesite, we released twenty-one doves into the sky as a representation of the Holy Spirit.

I prayed for Rita and Ashley because the loss was tragic, and God answered my prayer and responded miraculously on behalf of our family. God's grace and mercy brought us through the trade winds of life. He distinctively blessed our family with friends who love us.

They displayed their affections, generosity, and concerns for the welfare of our family during a pivotal time of despair. He covered us with blankets of love when we were at our weakest point. God blessed us while we mourned, and He took away some of the sting of death. He lifted our burdens and made our hearts glad. The power of prayer restored broken family relationships and made them whole again. God did not allow our family to desire revenge; instead, He replaced the loss with fond memories filled with joy and gladness.

God strengthened us when we became weary, and the renewed strength allowed us to smile instead of cry. We were able to stand tall and not faint, and we felt the presence and power of God endow our spirits. Prayer sustained our family through a difficult time of sorrow, and we are forever grateful for the hand of God moving in our lives. Although we missed Brian immensely, we were able to withstand the pain.

We apprehend clearly the effects of powerful prayers. These prayers transcend beyond human capabilities, comprehension, or expectations. Thank God for the power of prayer.

Power of Family Prayer

God loves families, and He instructs parents to teach their children how to pray. Family prayer is a profound dedication and reverence for God. The family essentially sets aside time to express their desires and concerns through prayer. They acknowledge God's holiness, and most importantly, identify their need for His involvement in their daily lives. My family prays at home, while we are traveling, and at church, or spontaneously. I pray for the Lord to keep my family out of harm's way. My prayer is for them to return home safely and to be protected from evil forces. From their departure until their arrival home, prayer is essential, for we do not know if they will return home safely.

I was watching the news, and the caption read, "Explosion at Shell Oil Refinery in Martinez, California." A hydrogen plant had exploded at Shell Oil Refinery due to a pipe rupturing. I listened attentively as the newscaster began to expound on the breaking news.

He said, "There is an explosion at Shell Oil Refinery in Martinez, California. The plant is being evacuated. Stay tuned for an update."

I was astonished! I felt palpitations in my heart because I remembered that my husband, Ronald, was working at Shell Oil Refinery. Thoughts raced through my mind: What happened? Was Ronald injured? How could I contact him at Shell Refinery? I prayed that God would protect him.

While I watched the plant engulfed with smoke on the television, I thought to myself, *This does not look good. Where is Ronald?* While I was watching the news, Ronald phoned to tell me he was unharmed. I was elated to hear his voice. Thank you, Jesus! Our prayers of protection were granted when I least expected it. God answers prayers timely, and because of our prayer petitions, God protected Ronald from the devastating fire.

Remember to pray for your family's protection consistently. Danger can occur any time, so pray with them and for them. Pray and ask God to be your surveillance camera. We need the Divine protection of God; therefore, exercise the prayer of faith that is deemed to work in our favor. God has given us the authority to ask anything in His name. Father, in the name of Jesus, send your guardian angels to protect, defend, and destroy every satanic scheme that our families may encounter. Amen.

Prayer for My Daughter

I vividly remember when my daughter, Shannon, called me from Nashville, Tennessee, concerning her classmate Omar, who has a medical history of epilepsy. She was frantic and asked me to contact his mother because Omar was in the emergency room at Metropolitan General Hospital in Nashville, Tennessee. Apparently, he was having frequent seizures.

I did not know Omar's mother; nevertheless, I agreed to call her and inform her of his condition. I dialed the phone number that Shannon gave me, but unfortunately, the automated service said, "You have reached a number that has been disconnected. Please check the number you have dialed or ask the operator for assistance." I phoned the operator, and she informed me that there was no one listed by that name. I then called my daughter to confirm the phone number.

Shannon said, "The number is correct."

I was very concerned because Omar was incoherent and unable to verify or correct the telephone number. Therefore, I told Shannon that I would connect with Omar's mother in the Spirit. I began to pray sincerely and asked God for Omar's mother to call and check on her son—and this prayer was answered spontaneously. Omar's mother phoned him on his cell phone while they were at the hospital. Shannon told her about his frequent seizures, and then asked her to contact me. Meanwhile, I was in El Sobrante, California, remaining prayerful, when Omar's mother called me from Los Angeles, California, to thank me for praying for her son. I was relieved to hear her voice and learn that Omar's condition was improving. God answers prayers in mysterious ways and leaves me in awe of His glory.

Never be reluctant to pray, regardless of the interference that you may encounter. The power of prayer reaches Heavenly dimensions that we are incapable of comprehending. Pursue prayer in every situation in your life. We often forget, but we should remember that the Holy Spirit assists us with our prayers as Jesus is interceding on our behalf. Wholesome prayer lives provide us with opportunities to draw on our faith when we face unbearable situations. Our problems should not suppress our faith; rather, faith should minimize our problems. Remember, our faith is the catalyst that drives our prayers to Heaven. We are not powerless; we are powerful because of the Holy Spirit. Battles are won through prayer because faith is the platform that we stand upon, heralding that "the just shall live by his faith" (Habakkuk 2:4 NKJV). Faith caused me to pray and proceed in the spiritual direction of God.

No matter what it appears like, God has control over every situation. He possesses the supernatural ability to change all resistance to comply with and conform to His plans. When you cannot visualize God, realize that you can rely on Him to remove opposition. Without prayer, our conditions remain unchanged, but remaining prayerful changes our circumstances and ultimate outcomes. Use prayer as a means to lift burdens that will ultimately destroy you.

God's desire is to see His power in you, and He has given you everything that you need to succeed.

CHAPTER FIVE

The Storm

"I said, 'Oh, that I had wings of a dove!
I would fly away and be at rest—
I would flee far away and stay in the desert; Selah
I would hurry to my place of shelter, far from the tempest and storm.'"
Psalm 55:6-8

It was a beautiful day for a family outing at California Great America located in Santa Clara, California. The sun was shining brilliantly, and the flowers were colorfully arranged in a beautiful design on a meticulously cut lawn. As we waited patiently in a lengthy line to get on the rides, my profuse perspiration startled my husband, and he insisted that we attend the movie theater because it was air-conditioned.

We all agreed and maneuvered our way through the crowd, arriving at the theater. As we entered, I stopped perspiring and felt relieved. It was very unusual for me to perspire profusely, and my family appeared very uncomfortable; even though they did not comment on what they had observed, they appeared puzzled. This symptom was the beginning of my thyroid storm.

One day, as I was driving down the street, I felt heart palpitations. I palpated my radial pulse, and my heart rate was 130 beats per minute. I was exhibiting signs of tachycardia (fast heartbeat). The next day, while I was working, I mentioned my symptoms to the charge nurse. She suggested I take my resting heart rate, because her daughter, Trianna, experienced symptoms of tachycardia and was diagnosed with thyroid disease. One night, while I was in bed, I palpated my wrist and counted my resting heart rate. It was 135 beats per minute. The next day, I contacted my physician to schedule an appointment.

As time progressed, my friends began to ask me if I was on a diet because I appeared to be losing weight; I assured them that I was not dieting. I weighed myself, and the scale verified that I had lost weight. I began to experience palpitations, edema around my eyes and ankles, dry skin, thinning hair, and lack of concentration—not to mention a thirty-pound weight loss. My heart would beat so loud, I could hear the pulsation in my ears. This symptom disturbed me greatly, so I resorted to sleeping upright in a chair to lessen the pounding sound in my ear, which was very unusual for me.

Thyroid Storm

My physician performed a routine examination, and he concluded that I was in a "thyroid storm." He performed lab tests, which confirmed the diagnosis of Graves' disease. He said, "Berney, you are in a thyroid storm." *I had never experienced a thyroid storm, and I seriously pondered what he said.* I have never been sick in my life, nor diagnosed with an incurable disease. I am a registered nurse, and I am the one who renders care to patients when they are incapable of caring for themselves. I typically console and encourage patients to get well, but now the roles were reversed, and I was the patient experiencing a storm and in need of medical attention.

Thyroid storms can be life-threatening and bring imminent danger. I thought to myself, *Get rid of every stressful situation in your life. From now on, focus on positive things and avoid negativism from disrupting your life.*

During this time, I was in litigation for an automobile accident, in which I was rear-ended and sustained a neck injury. Not only that, a long-term friendship was about to be broken, and now I was dealing with health issues. *Something must change!* I decided to hold on to everything that was good.

During the storm, I joined a church and rededicated my life to Christ. I learned to trust and depend on Jesus, and I began to pray heartfelt prayers. "Hear my cry, O God; listen to my prayer. From the ends of the earth I call to you, I call as my heart grows faint; lead me to the rock that is higher than I" (Psalm 61:1—2). I discovered God as the rock of my salvation; He is solid, stable, dependable, and sturdy.

Prayer Petition

I prayed, "LORD God Almighty, I am in unfamiliar territory, a thyroid storm, but I am leaning, depending, and trusting in you. As the Scripture says, "Anyone who trusts in him will never be put to shame" (Romans 10:11). I trust you, LORD! Now, LORD, I need You to cease the winds and the waves, for You are the Creator and Sustainer of the heavens and the earth and the sea below; no rushing wind, storm, or turbulent sea is greater than You. Now, LORD, speak—and the tempest storm shall cease! Speak, LORD—and peace will overcome the situation. Speak, LORD—and command the thyroid storm to flee. Command the antibodies to refrain from attacking my thyroid and turn back the process of the autoimmune disease. Inflammatory process, you've got to go! Thyroid-stimulating hormone, you shall return to normal. God created this mortal body out of dust, and He can demand it to conform to His will. Command the blood cells and immunoglobulins to obey You. My assurance is in You. Help me to overcome the stormy weather. Help your daughter visualize God's goodness in the midst of the storm. Help me overcome my disturbed state of mind. Have Your way, Oh God. Increase my faith until the storm ceases. Let this experience be a testimony for others. I give You the praise, honor, and glory, because You are the LORD that heals us (Exodus 15:26). Amen."

As I read the Bible, the culmination of my prayers and faith began to increase. I remember the Holy Spirit revealing to me to read Hebrews 11:1 (NKJV) that says, "Now faith is the substance of things hoped for, the evidence of things not seen." Faith is perceiving the movement of God when you are standing still; it is not a physical movement, but a spiritual encounter. I believed a miraculous event would occur from a supernatural God, and though I could not visualize a perceptible indication of my physical healing, I understand His ability to heal and bless me. And my faith is crucial to my healing. Hebrews 11:6 accentuates this point: "And without faith it is impossible to please God, because anyone who comes to him must believe that he exists and that he rewards those who earnestly seek him." God guarantees rewards to faithful people who persistently search for Him. I searched for God, and He provided me with answers. People who doubt His existence do not search for His answers; therefore, God is not pleased and they do not receive His blessing. While meditating on the verse from Hebrews, I wondered how much faith I really possessed. I knew God existed, but I was not walking with Him. My intention was not to become a replica of *faithlessness* but instead an example of *faithfulness*. I realized this transition could only occur from studying the Bible and applying biblical principles in my life, trusting God, and overcoming the thyroid storm.

It's Me, Oh Lord

Despite the turbulent conditions, I weathered the storm. I became more active in the church and joined the choir. One Sunday morning, the choir began to sing, "It's me, oh Lord, I'm standing in the need of prayer. Not my mother, father, sister, or brother, but it's me, oh Lord; I'm standing in the need of prayer." As I listened to the lyrics, I tried to sing along with the choir, but I soon realized that I needed prayer. I began to cry uncontrollably and the tears rushed down my face. The Holy Spirit was cleansing me, and I was becoming a new creature; God desired to see the reflection of Jesus through my purification. I did not understand why I was crying, but I knew God was moving profoundly in my life. I was being refined and experiencing a spiritual process of molding by the Potter. My rough edges, flaws, and stains were being spun away by God. He needed to reshape me to become Lord of my life and use me for the edification of the body of Christ. God reigns and rules in the heart of His people, and He was working within my heart and in my life, because I felt His presence; a spiritual renewal was stirring within me.

Church was dismissed, and I walked out the choir stand with tears streaming down my face. I did not speak to anyone while I was walking; I was completely engrossed, thinking about God's goodness. I did not understand everything the Holy Spirit was doing, but I realized something different was happening inside of me. I kept thinking about the song and prayer.

I recalled how people ask me to pray for their loved ones, friends, children, and coworkers, and I oblige because I realize prayer is necessary. But obviously, this time, I needed someone to pray for me. My family was concerned about my well-being, and so were my coworkers. My friends left messages and prayers on my phone, and when I heard their voices I cried, because I felt their compassion and perceived that they cared. My mother placed me on the prayer list at her church, and the congregation interceded for me in prayer. I confided in my mother and conveyed my concerns. I didn't know what I would do if I were unable to work as a registered nurse. She told me I had to take care of myself first before I could care for anyone else. I found myself crying out to God again in prayer. "But I call to God, and the Lord saves me. Evening, morning, and noon, I cry out in distress, and he hears my voice" (Psalm 55: 16—17). In my distress, I needed God; I was not ashamed to cry out to Him, because I trusted Him and needed Him to intervene in my life. Who else could I call on for assistance? Who hears my cry? No one but God. He is attentive to my voice! Expressing my feelings to Him gave me a sense of comfort. "How long will I endure sickness?" Only God knows.

Doctor's Visit

I spoke with Dr. Winton, a cardiologist with whom I worked closely. When I informed him of my symptoms, he was very concerned and asked me to walk downstairs to his office. His office was closed, but he personally scheduled in my appointment.

When we arrived, he looked sternly into my eyes and said, "Berney, keep this appointment; this is serious. Do you hear what I am saying?"

I replied, "Yes."

God was with me and gave me favor with the cardiologist; I'd received an appointment earlier than I anticipated. During my office visit, Dr. Winton obtained a history and physical, ordered an EKG, and prescribed anti-arrhythmic drugs to suppress my fast heart rate. My thyroid levels continued to fluctuate, so my primary physician scheduled me to receive radiation treatment. I continued to pray passionately and faithfully, learning how to trust God. I poured out my heart before the Lord and began to pray effectually as I drew closer to Him.

After the radiation treatment, my primary physician was having a difficult time trying to adjust my medication, so he referred me to an endocrinologist and a rheumatoidologist because my anti-nuclear antibody (ANA) blood test was elevated. My physician wanted me to be evaluated to rule out Systemic Lupus Erythrematosus. After I scheduled an appointment with the rheumatoidologist, he ruled out Systemic Lupus Erythrematosus. Hallelujah!

I then scheduled an appointment with the endocrinologist. During my office visit, the endocrinologist meticulously adjusted my medication and diagnosed me with Hashimoto's disease, an underactive thyroid gland condition known as hypothyroidism. I tried hard not to become overwhelmed with the ordeal. Nevertheless, I thought to myself what additional problems I would have to encounter. The anguish I felt about my medical problems concerned me, dearly. However, God sustained me through my distress. When anxiety was great within me, your consolation brought joy to my soul (Psalm 94:19). God removed my apprehension and uneasiness and instilled joy within my soul. Second Timothy 1:7 (NKJV) declares, "For God has not given us a spirit of fear, but of power and of love and of a sound mind." God had given me a sound mind to make sound decisions through the guidance of the Holy Spirit. As a result, I never lost hope and kept the faith as I fervently prayed.

My soul rejoiced exceedingly because of God's encouraging Words of comfort, and I blessed God because of who He is and what He has done for me. When stricken with disease, I worshipped God! When I was perplexed concerning the diagnosis, I praised God! When the physician ruled out Systemic Lupus Erythrematosus, I magnified God! Now I have learned to trust God immensely! My faith sustained me through the storm, and I know "many are the afflictions of the righteous, But the LORD delivers him out of them all" (Psalm 34:19 NKJV). He brings us through our afflictions to realize there is nothing impossible for God (Luke 1:37).

Whirlwind Storm

From my experience, I discovered that different types of storms can occur from natural phenomenon or physical ailment. The thyroid storm occurred suddenly in my life without warning and left evidence of destruction. While the tempest was raging in the storm of my life, the anchor of God kept me from capsizing. During the howling winds and ferocious storm, I felt God's presence. He shelters me from the elements capable of causing detriment.

When God rebuked the waters, they fled, and at the sound of Your thunder, they took flight (Psalm 104:7). God rebuked the turbulent waters in my life, and they ceased to flow. Why? God has dominion over nature. "You rule over the surging sea; when its waves mount up, you still them" (Psalm 89:9). He can calm the raging sea because he is "mightier than the thunder of the great waters, mightier than the breakers of the sea— the LORD on high is mighty!" (Psalm 93:4). He is mightier than His creation. Storms last for a moment in time, but God's presence and omnipotent power are everlasting.

The turbulence from the storm took a toll on my body, and the tempestuous winds left evidence of destruction, but Jesus said, "Peace, be still!" God speaks with power and authority; His word captivates His creation's attention, and an imminent sense of calmness exists. He stilled the storm to a whisper; the waves of the sea were hushed (Psalm 107:29). Jesus is the Prince of Peace and His supernatural power has supremacy over nature. Jesus is a deliverer; I discovered Him to be my refuge and strength during troublesome times. Jesus is my living hope, the lifeline to my soul, and my hope has always been—and will forever be—in the Lord God Almighty!

From my experience, I learned that tribulations accompany storms. My tribulations tested my faith and redefined my character. Enduring the storm has taught me to persevere, regardless of any disappointment or frustration that I've encountered. God empowered me to soar like an eagle above the raging waters. He renewed my strength with His grace and mercy, and I was able to withstand the storm. By His restoration power, the Lord prevented me from becoming overwhelmed, and the outpouring of His love enabled me to testify about the goodness of the Lord. He is my Lord and Savior, anchor, refuge, and great physician.

Thunder Storm

After my storm ceased, my nephew Larry Dorton Jr. was diagnosed with thyroid disease and renal failure. He died from complications from the surgery. He was 25 years old. Our hearts were grief-stricken. Personally, I felt I could have died from thyroid complications, but God did not allow this to happen. In my distress, I called to the Lord, petitioning Him in prayer and asking Him about the purpose of my life. One day while I was at the altar, God revealed to me that my purpose was to "do good." It is excellent in my sight and profitable for everyone (Titus 3:8). Devote yourself to perform good deeds.

I finally realized what God was trying to convey to me: "Berney, continue to pray fervently, help people who are in need, continue to be there for the people who mourn, visit the people who are incarcerated, stand up for righteousness, encourage people who are disappointed, and continue to be a guiding light in a dark world. Pray for your family and the household of faith. Minister to my people; when you do good, you represent me as an ambassador of Christ. Berney, continue to be a servant, take care of the sick, and pray for those who are in need. Be mindful that you possess the powerful gift of healing. You have the powerful gifts of prophecy and discernment—use them to edify the Body of Christ. Remain prayerful."

Grateful Prayer

God, I am grateful that you revealed to me the purpose of my life. Order my steps in Your Word, God; etched are Your Word on the doorpost of my heart and soul. I will not sin against You. Father, help me to be the ambassador of Christ that I desire to become. Help me to minister as a passionate flame of fire to a perishing world. Ignite the fire so the flames can become intense. Let Your Kingdom prevail against the kingdom of darkness that is the prince of this earth. Help me to be the guiding light; let my light shine so that man can see the "good work" that You have bestowed in me. Let my life be a living sacrifice and testimony about the goodness of the Lord, emulating your essence. I pray honestly and fervently that you will prevail in every aspect of my life, allowing me to grow in grace and favor. Send anointed and appointed vessels willing to assist me with prayer and ministry, and empower us to save souls, change lives, reunite families, and restore marriages by the power of the Holy Spirit. I pray these things in Jesus' precious name and I consider it done. In the blessed name of Jesus, amen.

CHAPTER SIX

Prayerfully Weathering the Storm

"Come, for everything is now ready."
Luke 14:17

Operational Storm

My son and I entered the entrance of the hospital, and the nursing supervisor gave us a cordial greeting, saying, "Everything has been arranged for Andre. When he returns from surgery, his room will be located on the third floor, adjacent to the nursing station." Her statement resonated in my spirit, confirming to me that Andre's surgery would be successful. As we rode the elevator to the third floor, she continued to explain the admission procedures. Andre was very quiet and reserved, though I knew a million questions were racing through his mind, but he remained calm. Andre was experiencing symptoms of bleeding and abdominal pain. His lab work was abnormal, and the lab results indicated that he had low hemoglobin.

When we arrived at his room, the nursing staff began to admit him to the hospital and prepare him for surgery. When he looked into my eyes for reassurance, I assured him that everything was going to be all right. I worked at the hospital in the Medical Intensive Care Unit, and I was familiar with the admission procedures, as well as the staff.

As the nurse continued to prepare him for surgery, I phoned my husband to inform him of our son's hospitalization and scheduled operation. Unfortunately, I was unable to contact him because he had not arrived home from work. I phoned the church to ask the church members to pray for Andre, but no one was available. No one knew about his admission to the hospital for emergency surgery.

Without hesitation, I began to pray for God to guide the surgeon's hand. "God, I know that You are the Great Physician who possesses healing virtue. You are the great "I Am." Lord, right now I need You to be the Chief Surgeon in the operating room. Just like the woman with the issue of blood, heal the area where bleeding exists. Whatever way You decide to bless Andre, I'll be satisfied. It is in Your miraculous, marvelous, majestic name that healing takes place, and I give You praise, honor, and glory. God, I thank You in advance for answering my prayer. Amen."

The orderly wheeled Andre's gurney into the surgery room. Meanwhile, I sat in his room, reflecting back on when he was a little boy and complained of abdominal pain. I noticed that he would eat dinner, then immediately go to the bathroom. I discussed his behavior with my husband and explained my concern regarding Andre's ability to absorb his food. I scheduled an appointment with a gastroenterologist, and they performed a colonoscopy and endoscopy. After the procedure was completed, tissues from his stomach were sent to the lab for a biopsy. The physician informed me that the biopsy results confirmed that Andre had Crohn's disease, which is an incurable autoimmune disease. After I consulted with his physicians, I went home and discussed the results with Andre and my husband. I then asked Andre to describe his symptoms.

He said, "I always have pain when I have a bowel movement, and occasionally cramping pain in my stomach. I thought it was normal."

I discussed with him the reasons why his symptoms occurred, explaining why he would have to take medication for the rest of his life (the medication was to prevent inflammation and abdominal pain). All of this news was overwhelming for a sixteen-year-old teenager.

Andre was having difficulty complying with taking his medicine; the pills made him gain weight, and that bothered him. I tried to reassure him that the medication would prevent him from having problems with inflammation and stomach cramps, but his reluctance to take the medication continued.

Crohn's Flare-up

Andre appeared to be doing fine, until one day when he phoned me from summer school and told me he was having severe abdominal pain and bleeding. I immediately phoned his physician, who told me to bring him to his office. The physician examined Andre and collected lab work, the results of which were abnormal. He scheduled an appointment for Andre to have a colonoscopy procedure. The physician (gastroenterologist) discovered that Andre had a fistula, and he decided to admit him to the hospital for surgery.

I waited patiently in Andre's room for him to return from surgery, and while I was there, God's presence in the room reassured me that everything was going to be all right. The Bible declares, "Those who know your name will trust in you, for you, LORD, have never forsaken those who seek you" (Psalm 9:10). I trust God wholeheartedly. God, I know Your name! You are Yahweh, Jehovah Shalom, El Shaddai, Emmanuel, Jehovah Roeh, Jehovah Jireh, Adonai, Jehovah Tsidkenu, and Jehovah Elyon. Most importantly, You are the great "I Am"; You are anything that You want to be, and I am delighted that I can call upon Your name with reverence and honor.

LORD, I know I am blessed because of my trust in You. God, I will always trust in You with all my heart. God, I love You with all my mind, body, and soul. Thank You for directing me not to lean to my own understanding. Thank You for letting the Holy Spirit guide me to truth. Lord, it was You directing our pathway as we entered and exited the hospital corridor. I appreciate and acknowledge You for all You have done and continue to do for my son and our family. I bless Your name, for You are good, and Your mercy endures forever. You are the true and living God! When I called Your name, Majesty, You answered my prayer spontaneously. God, Your reassurance, peace, and love comforted me in the room, and I felt serene because of the presence of the Holy Spirit. Thank You for Your loving kindness.

The surgery was successful, and the surgeon informed me that Andre was in the recovery room. My son and I had received a bountiful blessing from the Lord; God arranged for Andre's surgery to proceed without incident. The Lord foreknew that Andre was going to have a successful surgery, and the preparation was orchestrated by a Divine and loving God. From Andre's entrance into the hospital to his exit out of the surgery room, God's master plan prevailed. He prepared the surgeons and nurses to care for my son with compassion.

Thank you, God, for taking care of my child during the operational storm.

Stormy Weather

Unpredictable storms arise in everyone's lives, destroying livelihoods, hopes, and dreams. Storms confront our psychological, physical, and spiritual stability. They occur when:

- The doctor explains, "You have six months to live."
- You receive a frightening phone call explaining that your husband has been in an automobile accident.
- You receive a foreclosure letter about your home.
- You receive a termination notice from your job.
- Someone burglarizes your home.
- Ungodly men gang-rape your daughter.
- You grieve over the death of a love one.

When you experience a storm, it feels like the ship is sinking and the lifeboat is missing. Some people experience a sense of doom and desperation; they internalize their agony and discover solutions to their problems that are essentially farfetched. We are incapable of contending with storms unless Jesus is aboard; He is the captain of the ship and the answer to our problems. When the disciples encountered a fierce storm, they called on Jesus; their faith took a backseat to fear, and desperation took control. They even went so far as to question Jesus, "Do you not care if we perish?" But Jesus secured the ship and saved the disciples' lives. The disciples were not destined to die on the ship; their fate resided with Jesus, not the storm.

Are you in a storm? Where winds howl and the rain falls consistently? Are you riding the swells of the waves, crying out to God? Are you fearful for your life? Never hesitate to call upon the Lord for His assistance. Our recourse is God! Ask Him, "God where are you?" He is the anchor that prevents winds from battering us through the raging storm.

When nothing makes sense, don't reason with yourself; trust God. Trust Him when you cannot see Him. Call on Him when you desire a response. Turn your thoughts and anguish over to Him. Seize the opportunity to concentrate on God rather than distort the problem. Do not panic; instead, pray until the situation changes. Remain prayerful when you are discouraged, and pray for discernment not to sabotage God's plan. Maintain spiritual integrity with God to broaden your insight about the problem, and He will help you cope with the situation. God is with us! God is the weatherman in the storm who foretells the forecast. Do not become emotionally distraught; evaluate the situation spiritually.

Storms bring us to the pinnacle of grace; they reveal our faith to God, as well as His attributes to us. David said it was good that he was afflicted. Without affliction, man would not search for God; he would rather rely on his strength instead of God's power. God teaches us how to operate in the midst of the whirlwind to overcome the problem, instead of allowing it to overwhelm us. Stormy situations never determine our course of action, only God does.

Faith in the Storm

As an attempt to undermine their faith, fear has confronted the most devout Christians. During storms, we sense imminent danger, and that is when our faith should extract fear and infuse hope. The real fear is not the storm, but lack of faith. Our objective is to maneuver from fear to reliance on God. Abort fear and activate faith. We walk by faith and not by sight. Our faith walk does not rely on our sight, but rather on our spiritual discernment.

God will not allow us to sink to the bottom of the sea or become shipwrecked; instead, He tests our faith. Storms challenge our faith and test our characters. James declares that our faith increases during trials. Faith is a character builder that perfects our weaknesses, and joy transcends when faith is activated. During trials, faith flourishes instead of becoming stagnant. Maximize your faith to minimize the problem. Walk forward in faith instead of backwards in fear. Faithfully proclaim God's promises. I will bless the Lord at all times, and His praises shall continually be in my mouth. God has not forgotten how to bless His people. You should not forget how to bless God—especially during storms! Give thanks in everything; praise helps determine the outcome of your storm.

Our most precarious positions are in storms. Do not look at the waves; instead, focus on Christ. He will give you the fortitude to walk on the water (like Peter) as He ceases the winds and waves. Our mental and spiritual stability should never waver during a storm. Endure the storm with courage; it is only a temporary imposition. High tides will come, but you have the ability to ride the waves. The current may be compelled to take you in a different direction, but God is the anchor that stabilizes your position, and prayer is the ship that takes us to the shore.

God's directions are precise as He navigates us to safety. Jesus stills the storm for us to regain peace in our lives. If you are going through a storm, count it all joy; God is testing your faith. Jesus is not afraid of storms, and neither should you be. He rebukes storms, allowing peace to emerge and turbulence to subside. Look for the rainbow that represents God's promise. Pray for God to refine your character, increase your faith, and change your mindset. Ask God what lesson He desires you to learn from the situation. Does He want you to swim, sit, or walk on water? It is apparent that He does not want you to complain. Fear not! God is with you. You can have peace in the midst of the storm.

Father God, in the name of Jesus, the tempest is raging. Help us not to drown and to stay afloat. Help us not to dread the storm; instead, teach us how to ride the waves to shore. Give us the tenacity to withstand the storm. Turn the forceful winds in your direction. Take away the fear factor and infuse us with great faith. Thank You for peace, which soothes our souls, comforts our minds, and transcends all understanding.

CHAPTER SEVEN

Divine Interventions

"Then Abraham approached him and said: "Will you sweep away the righteous with the wicked?"
Genesis 18:23

Abraham, a prayerful man, is well acquainted with divine interventions. God's anger burned against Sodom and Gomorrah because of their atrocious sins, which warranted God's judgment. He instructed angels to destroy both cities. Lot, Abraham's nephew, was an inhabitant of Sodom. Because he did not want Lot to die due to the other inhabitants' perverseness, Abraham reverently inquired of God to reconsider the fate of Sodom and Gomorrah. He reminded God that righteous people deserve justice and ungodly people deserve His wrath. God granted mercy towards Lot's family instead of condemnation, and angels ushered Lot's family out of a doomed city. They all escaped Sodom's destruction—except for Lot's wife, who turned into a pillar of salt because she looked back.

Destruction comes when sins are flagrant, but blessings remain upon the righteous. God blessed Abraham's family because of his persistence. His family received God's favor in spite of their predicament. Perverse actions of ungodly people are capable of causing detriment to the righteous, but divine intervention causes God to reconsider His judgment.

Moses intervened for the children of Israel after they became corrupt and made a golden calf in the wilderness. They began to worship and make sacrifices to a graven image, and that was despicable to God. They disobeyed the commandment that says, "I am the LORD your God, who brought you out of Egypt, out of the land of slavery. You shall have no other gods before me" (Exodus 20:2—3). Idolatry ignited the anger of God, and the Israelites provoked the Lord's wrath. Moses, though, found favor in the Lord by defusing God's anger and reminding Him of His omnipotent power and authority. God's anger dissipated, and the Lord had compassion on the stiff-necked Israelites. Moses' prayers prevented God from committing genocide and exterminating the entire Jewish nation.

Abigail fell at David's feet, intervening for the lives of her husband and their male servants. She reminded David that vengeance comes from the Lord. Her persuasiveness deterred David from murdering her wicked husband (Nabal) and their male servants. David praised God for Abigail's keen perception of the problem. Her divine intervention saved Nabal's life and blessed her household and David's men.

In our society, God still searches for men and women who are available to be used for divine interventions. God, who specifically instructs Christians to become involved in the welfare of others, orchestrates their involvement. These people aggressively pray, intercede, or protect others from unforeseen circumstances and warn them of God's judgments.

Spiritual Deposit

Our family was sitting at the dinner table watching a television program, when suddenly a news bulletin interrupted the television broadcast, informing us of a breaking news report about a Brinks employee who had been shot and killed in Berkeley, California. We listened and watched attentively as the news reporter told the story. The caption on the television read, "Breaking News: A Brinks employee shot at a local bank." A young woman employed by Brinks Company was the victim of an armed robbery. As the story unfolded, it became apparent that the perpetrators followed the armored truck, and when she got out of the truck, they shot and killed her at the scene. This devastating news shocked our family—especially our son Andre—because earlier that day, the Brinks employee and a coworker had made a delivery of cash to the bank where Andre was employed.

The news stunned her coworkers. They were overwhelmed with grief and several employees resigned, while others took a stress leave. Andre thought the incident that occurred in Berkeley, California, could also happen at the branch where he was employed, so he expected the branch manager to implement security measures to ensure the safety of the employees. Would their employer comply? He was uncertain of their plans and the tragic event traumatized the employees, and Andre feared for his life. He comprehended that his working environment was unsafe, and that defining moment changed his perspective concerning his job. He recognized that their plight was in God's hands, not man's, and that this cumbersome situation needed God's assistance. Therefore, he asked me if I would come and pray at the bank where he worked. I agreed to come on my day off.

As I prepared to visit the bank, I thought to myself, *I am not a customer at this bank.* Nonetheless, I had a purpose to fulfill. When I arrived at the bank, I anointed the door where the customers entered and the counter where the customers prepared their deposit slips. I stalled because I wanted to concentrate on praying without appearing obvious. As I continued to pray, I prayed for the customers' safety. God answered my prayers, and I stood in line behind the customers while I anointed the ropes where they stood, waiting to be served by the tellers.

Andre saw me in line and smiled. I thought to myself, *This bank has surveillance cameras, and I do not have any transaction to make.* Passing a note to the tellers would raise suspicion, and I did not want to attract attention to myself, nor did I want them to think that it was a robbery. The Holy Spirit quickly reminded me why I was there—to make a deposit in prayer, anoint the building, and allow the Holy Spirit to protect the employees and customers from the evil forces that had taken the woman's life. In light of the spiritual warfare, I realized that intercessory prayer was the divine transaction that I was depositing in the bank.

I stood in line, patiently praying and smiling as I allowed several customers to go ahead of me to make their transactions. The teller then said, "Next in line."

As I approached the teller window, I touched the countertop and saw that the teller was my son.

I said, "Good evening."

Andre responded and said, "Good evening." He then introduced me to the teller in the next booth. She asked me to pray for her, and I complied with her request. The expressions on Andre and his co-worker's faces were heartfelt, and the sparkle in their eyes conveyed to me their thankfulness and appreciation for the prayers.

Because of the violence many people encounter in this world, strength and courage are essential to taking a stance to repel violent crimes. God allowed me to walk forcefully and aggressively against demonic forces—"not by might nor by power, but by my Spirit, says the LORD Almighty" (Zechariah 4:6). The Spirit of God raises up a standard to derail demonic attacks, and the Holy Spirit empowers saints to regain and restore order while executing dominance against the enemy. "I have given you authority to trample on snakes and scorpions and to overcome all the power of the enemy; nothing will harm you" (Luke 10:19). God's resurrected power incapacitates Satan from harming us as He empowers us with the insurmountable faith to accomplish the tasks He has assigned us to perform.

God has placed a hedge of protection around the bank that bulletproof windows cannot accomplish. No robberies or altercations have occurred from 1996 to the present time, 2011. Praise the LORD! I victoriously walked out of the bank, acknowledging essential components of Divine intervention. These include obedience, faithfulness, prayer, and spiritual warfare.

God has made a spiritual deposit within us to accomplish phenomenal victories, and this experience has taught me a valuable lesson. God equips you with everything you need to complete the assignment. Most importantly, spiritual deposits are guaranteed for a lifetime and yield high earnings from God.

Obedience to God's Word

"Talented and pretty" describes Britney. She plays the drums at our church and announced to the congregation one Sunday that she had entered a beauty pageant. The Lord revealed to me that she would win the contest if she did *three* things: (1) prayed before she arrived at the pageant; (2) prayed while she was riding in the car; and (3) prayed prior to her performance on the drums. The next Sunday, I looked for Britney, but she did not attend church. I spoke to Azariah (her mom) about what the Lord had told me, and she asked me to call Britney. I phoned Britney and told her what the Lord had said, and she listened attentively.

When the day of the pageant arrived, I wanted to know if she had won. My children and I were watching movies and I looked at the clock; it was midnight. I told Andre to call her.

He said, "Mom, it is late." I told him to call Britney that they had probably just arrived home from the pageant.

My children looked at me inquisitively and said, "How do you know if she just arrived home?"

I said, "The Holy Spirit revealed it to me." They complied and called Britney. Azariah answered the phone.

We were excited and asked, "Did Britney win?"

Elated, Azariah exclaimed, "Yes!"

I picked up the phone and asked her if the building had steps.

She said, "Yes."

I was in awe! The Lord had revealed to me that the building had three steps. God allowed me to prophesy to Britney about His instructions, and He ultimately blessed her with a college scholarship because of her obedience and my discernment of the Holy Spirit.

The Holy Spirit's Instructions

"Will you not revive us again, that your people may rejoice in you?" (Psalm 85:6). Our church revival was exhilarating! The *Shekinah* glory of the Lord was present and the music was spiritually electrifying. The lead singer had a harmonious angelic voice that touched our hearts and convicted us of our sins. People's hands were raised in adoration of God, shouting Hallelujah and dancing with praise. I wondered why I was not engaged in this anointed worship experience. Instead of being a worshipper, I was a spectator. As I sat nervously on the edge of the pew, I took a panoramic view of the congregation. People were weeping uncontrollably, shouting, and rejoicing in the Lord. I was in awe of what I visualized in the spiritual realm. The Holy Spirit revealed to me that the lead singer was in spiritual warfare, and that Satan desired to destroy his life because of his talent and ability to touch the hearts of God's people.

God profoundly spoke to me, and the Holy Spirit confirmed His message. I had never before encountered such a profound spiritual revelation. His message was simple, clear, and precise: tell the church to pray for him. I thought to myself, *Does God want me to stop the service or alert the pastor? Should I tell the congregation, "What thus says the Lord?"* Thoughts were rushing through my mind. *What will the people think? Should I disrupt service now?* The more I procrastinated, the stronger the Holy Spirit spoke. I became uncomfortable and starting squirming in my seat, vacillating between leaving my seat and waiting to hear further instructions from the Lord. I continued to observe the congregation rejoicing in the spirit.

I felt an intense urgency to relay the message, but I did not know how. I felt like Jeremiah when he declared, "His word is in my heart like a fire, a fire shut up in my bones, I am weary of holding it in; indeed, I cannot" (Jeremiah 20:9). I thought to myself, *How long can I sit here without delivering the message?* My intent was not to be disobedient to God, but instead to figure out a way to communicate the message. I immediately removed a pen and paper from my purse and began to write a note to the young man (as if I were taking dictation from the Holy Spirit). Literally, I was. I wrote everything that God and the Holy Spirit had prompted me to write, and I advised him to read specific Scriptures because he was in spiritual warfare. I wrote down the Scriptures, chapters, and the verses and I informed him that I would be praying for him. When church adjourned, I sprinted through the congregation to deliver the note to his wife, as if I were Yusan Bolt, asking her to give the note to her husband and tell him that I was praying for him. After I delivered the message, I felt relieved; it was as if a ton of bricks had been lifted off my shoulders.

I learned from that encounter that spiritual warfare is present during high praise. God intercedes for His people in mysterious ways, regardless of whether we are walking with Him or turning away from Him. He is sovereign and possesses power that protects people from dangerous situations. He gives us explicit directives to follow, and He warns people of impending doom and destruction in order to prevent Satan from destroying their lives or sifting them like wheat.

I spoke with this young man's cousin, and she confirmed that he was experiencing spiritual warfare with drugs.

Preparing for a Battle

My sister, niece, and I were preparing the funeral arrangements for my deceased mother with the funeral director. When he left the room for a moment to photocopy some documents, we began to pray as we waited for him to return. After we prayed, the spirit of the Lord spoke to us, saying, "Rebuke and destroy the spiritual darkness of drug addiction." This stronghold was present in a relative's life, and we needed to confront him. We looked at each other and agreed that after we completed our business transaction with the funeral director, we would go to the relative's apartment.

The funeral director returned and asked us if everything was all right because he had overheard us praying and shouting "Hallelujah!" He told us that he was also a Christian, as he sat quietly to let us compose ourselves before proceeding with the funeral arrangements.

After our business transaction, we drove to our relative's apartment. We realized that God's divine appointment entailed spiritual warfare and that the demons of drugs would be exposed by the power of the Holy Ghost.

We walked gallantly to the apartment and anointed the doorknob with oil. Then we knocked on the door like the Drug Enforcement Agency—bang, bang, bang, bang!

The person behind the screen door asked, "Who is it?"

I said, "Berney."

After we identified ourselves, they let us inside the apartment. The pungent odor of crack cocaine permeated the entire apartment. I swiftly walked directly to the back room, and my niece (Kimberly) began to minister about God to the woman who was in the front room. The woman was wearing her hospital bracelet on her arm and apparently had been recently released from the hospital. We learned she had been diagnosed with AIDS. She still indulged in smoking crack cocaine, but when my niece witnessed to her about the Lord, she began to cry as she raised her hands up in the air in a surrendering position.

The people in the back room fled when I told them to come out of the room. Deuteronomy 28:7 proclaims, "The LORD will grant that the enemies who rise up against you will be defeated before you. They will come at you from one direction but flee from you in seven." We honestly witnessed the enemy escaping from different rooms in the apartment. This Scripture reveals to us the awesome power of God. We were strategically placed in the enemy's camp, and we were not afraid. It was an incredible experience! God exposed the enemy's darkness with His prophetic Word, which brings light and life to the soul.

The Lord was with us as He took control. James 4:7 proclaims, "Submit yourselves, then, to God. Resist the devil, and he will flee from you." Everyone in the apartment stopped what they were doing and listened to what thus said the LORD. We were obedient to the Holy Spirit and bold in our actions, and God strengthened us to confront the demonic spirit of drug addiction.

In the funeral home, God orchestrated an extraordinary Divine intervention capable of baffling the minds of many saints. We never questioned God; instead, we acted upon His directives. I had never before been involved with a spiritual assignment that entails the strategic tactic of actually going to the enemy's camp. Christian's objective is to denounce, rebuke, tear down, and annihilate the power of the prince of this world and everything that does not represent God. We aggressively war against Satan to establish and reclaim lives destroyed by his deceptive tactics, and our mission is explicit: to overthrow the kingdom of Satan while building up the kingdom of God.

Divine interventions are spiritual plans designed by God. He orchestrates Divine intervention to assist people who are in need of encouragement, deliverance, and blessings. God explicitly uses people to intervene on behalf of others, irrespective of the events that are occurring in our lives. The Holy Spirit quickens us to respond appropriately to God's call, and we proceed with caution, being wise as serpents and gentle as doves. God instructed me to intervene for my family, coworkers, and church by rebuking the bondage of addiction, and guidance from the Holy Spirit encouraged me to be courageous and fearless.

Obedience to the Holy Spirit makes us mindful of God's instructions. A special anointing happens when God gives us assignments, wisdom, and power to execute authority. Do not be perturbed by questioning yourself whether God is speaking to you. His sheep know His voice; therefore, proceed accordingly. We are equipped to deploy weapons intended to ignite, arrest, and combat evil. God is willing to send saints on strategic assignments that He can trust. Therefore, pray that God will use you for a "Divine intervention" that will help others and bless your life.

Father God, in the name of Jesus, thank You for appointing saints to intervene on behalf of others who are oblivious to their plights. You anoint people who diligently desire to build God's kingdom and annihilate spiritual wickedness. Empowerment enables them to intervene swiftly and refrain from hindering their flesh through demonic forces. Their position is not happenstance, but rather appointed by You. I bless Your name for choosing me as a vessel to intervene on behalf of others. Help me to understand the importance of the assignment and to never waver in my stance. Keep me humble. May Your power always be evident in my life.

Divine interventions are necessary, to expose harmful situations, reveal blessings, and provide protection to endangered people. Someone intervened on my behalf. Lord, I thank You for heeding their call. Hallelujah! Impress upon the minds of the saints to be ready, willing, and able to hearken to Your voice. No matter what the situation entails, we know and have an assurance that God is with us; He will never leave us nor forsake us. You are the rod and staff that comfort us and deliver us from evil. Let us proceed in the power of the Holy Spirit, which richly indwells within our souls.

Thank You for sending us and seeing the potential in us to intervene for others, to pray with them and for them, encourage them, strengthen them, and instruct them in spiritual truth. Help us to maintain our spiritual integrity and zeal for righteousness. You receive the glory from all our lives, and we will continue to pray in faith. In Jesus' name, I pray, amen.

CHAPTER EIGHT

Prayerful During Death

"Yea, though I walk through the valley of the shadow of death,
I will fear no evil;
for You are with me;
Your rod and Your staff, they comfort me."
Psalm 23:4 (NKJV)

My Mother's death was a low point in my life. God's presence revealed a remarkable peace that comforted me throughout the grieving process and instilled strength that helped me not to fear death, but instead to embrace His love. The valley experience helped me to walk confidently and grow spiritually. Fear was never a factor, but God's agape (love) was the essential element that helped me to walk through the valley and the shadow of death. Mother died suddenly, and I boldly cried out to the Lord in prayer. I always dreaded thinking about my mother's demise. How would our family cope? Would we argue over her possessions? Would we effectively communicate and become closer or become bitter with resentment towards one another?

When I would discuss making a last will and testament with my mother she would always change the subject nonchalantly, which would trouble me. It was an uncomfortable topic, but I felt we needed to discuss her plans. I wanted her to write her will and inform her children of her final wishes regarding her possessions. I discussed my concerns with her, telling her that a will would make grieving a lot easier if we foreknew her plans. One day, my greatest fear came true.

The hysterical phone call I received from my sister about my mother's death is etched in my memory forever.

My coworker said, "Berney, telephone."

I answered the phone and said, "Same Day Surgery, Berney speaking."

The frantic woman on the telephone screamed, repeatedly shouting, "My mother is dead! My mother is dead! My mother is dead!"

I repeated what she said. "Your mother is dead!"

I didn't recognize the voice of the distraught woman speaking to me on the phone. I later realized that it was my sister, Mary.

She then replied, "Our mother is dead!"

I said, "Who is this?"

She replied, "Mary, our mother is dead, and she is lying on the floor in her apartment—get here quickly!"

I could not believe what I was hearing. My mother did not have any history of cardiovascular disease, cancer, diabetes, respiratory disease, or renal failure. I tried to figure out what the cause of death could be. Was she having symptoms that she did not communicate to us? Was the cause of death from myocardial infarction, or arrhythmia? I could not fathom what I had just heard. Overhearing the conversation, my coworkers looked at me in what appeared to be shock. The blank expression that I returned to them let them know that I, too, was shocked.

They stared at me with compassion and were at a loss for words. Although they wanted to embrace me, they did not know how I would react.

They said, "It is okay, Berney; you can leave now."

I remembered I did not have transportation to my mother's apartment because my husband had taken my car to the shop. I phoned our children and told them to come to their grandmother's apartment. After my conversation with my children, my coworker Barbara, offered to drive me to my mother's apartment, and I graciously accepted. A million thoughts were raging through my mind. I kept thinking that my mother was in good health and she was not ill. She faithfully visited her physician for her annual physical and follow-up appointments, and she religiously followed her diet regimen.

As I rode in the car with Barbara, I said, "My mom is in good health." I could not remember the rest of the conversation, but I was trusting God. As we arrived at my mom's apartment, I saw the ambulance parked in her driveway, and a cold chill passed throughout my body. I quickly opened up the car door and sprinted up the stairs to her apartment. As I entered the door, my brother, sister, and the ambulance attendants were in her apartment. I passed by my brother, who was sitting on the sofa in the living room with his head in his hands. My sister was in the bedroom, saying, "Oh, Lord." I went to Mom's bedroom and saw her lifeless body lying face down on the floor with a beige blanket placed over her back. I kneeled down beside her, touched her cold mottled body, and said, "Momma," but I knew she was dead. When I touched her, I knew she no longer occupied that mortal body. I felt like every ounce of blood had been drawn out of me.

I asked my sister what happened, and she began to explain that, on Wednesday night, Mother had said that she was going to take a bath and lie down because she was not feeling well; apparently, she was experiencing pain in her hip. My sister and brother had called her on Thursday morning and Thursday evening, but she did not respond. On Friday morning, they entered her apartment and discovered her body on the floor, cold and lifeless. They called the ambulance, whose attendants pronounced her dead. We noticed that the bath water was drawn and a white towel was in the water, but apparently, she never took her bath.

I began to thank God because our mother was saved. The Bible proclaims that to be absent from the body is to be present with the Lord. Although her remains were lying on the floor, our mother's spirit was present with the Lord. The water in the tub was symbolic to me because water represents the Holy Spirit. She had thrown in the white towel to this troubled world, her children, friends, and church members, which represented a surrendering and purified spirit. Now she is spending a lifetime with Jesus, the one who bore all of her sins. She no longer needs to take a physical bath because she has been spiritually cleansed and washed by the blood of Jesus.

I tried to analyze everything I had to do. We began to make preparations for the funeral. We contacted her sisters in Beaumont, Texas, to inform them of her death. I phoned Aunt Rose, and I knew the news would devastate her because she had recently lost her husband (Uncle George) and was grieving over his death.

When I phoned and gave Aunt Rose the shocking news, she began to cry and said, "No one was with her; she died alone." As she wept, it broke my heart to hear her cry. My mother was her oldest sister, and her untimely death only compounded Aunt Rose's grief. I thought about what she had said, that Mom had "died alone," and it saddened me dearly. The Holy Spirit brought to my remembrance what the Bible says, "For I am convinced that neither death nor life, neither angels nor demons, neither the present nor the future, nor any powers, neither height nor depth, nor anything else in all creation, will be able to separate us from the love of God that is in Christ Jesus our Lord" (Romans 8:38—39).

My mother was not alone during the final hour of her life, and death did not separate her from the love of God that is in Christ Jesus. God is omnipresent and omniscient; He was with her in her apartment. The Scripture proclaims, "Precious in the sight of the LORD is the death of his saints" (Psalm 116:15). His agape love embraced and welcomed her into the eternal kingdom of God. Eternal life is a promise from God to all Christians, and I am grateful to know that I can stand on God's word and His promises. He reassures us that death is not the end. "Even in death the righteous have a refuge" (Proverb 14:32). Hallelujah! Christ Jesus is our refuge! Heaven is our home. Moreover, the saint's inheritance is reserved in heaven and will never perish, spoil, or fade.

Death is an imminent part of life, and family members grieve while experiencing bewilderment, which often puts them in a state of shock. Our tears release the sorrow that we feel internally, but death is the destiny of every man; the living should take this to heart

(Ecclesiastes 7:2). Death occurs because of man's sin, but there is a greater gain when the mortal life is over—a spiritual and eternal destination for Christians is to be with Jesus Christ. Solomon asserts, "There is a time for everything and a season for every activity under heaven, a time to be born and a time to die" (Ecclesiastes 3:1—2). We rejoice when a child is born into the world, but when death occurs we are exceedingly sorrowful because of the loss. Death is certain, and the finality of death closes the chapter on our lives. The Bible explains, "man is destined to die once, and after that to face judgment" (Hebrews 9:27). Just like an hourglass, our time will elapse because we are destined to die.

As our family waited for the coroner, police, and mortuary to pick up our mother's remains, there was a calmness in her apartment. The Bible emphasizes that those who are led by the spirit are sons of God. The Holy Spirit led our mother to glory, and the Holy Spirit quickens us to pray. God knows what we are in need of prior to our asking. Our family acknowledged in prayer that we needed His Divine guidance and strength because the matriarch of the family had departed. After we prayed, the coroner released the body, and the mortuary came and picked up Mom's remains. Their professionalism impressed me as they extended their condolences to our family. They asked the family if we wanted to remain in the room, and we responded, "Yes." They reassured us that they would take care of the arrangements for our mother, and we agreed to schedule an appointment to discuss her funeral arrangements.

After this ordeal was over, we did not apprehend exactly where to begin. Looking for her insurance policies, we searched her closet and rifled through her belongings. While searching through her closet, we discovered that all of her business was in order. She demonstrated to all of us how finances should be kept. Every receipt for her rent, utilities, insurances, phone, and credit cards bills was meticulously in order. She kept a receipt book to indicate whether she paid by cash, money order, or credit card. She had also written explicit instructions about her funeral arrangements and her possessions. She emphasized the importance of maintaining unity within the family, refraining from arguing, and "doing good." I was amazed at how meticulously she conducted her business. How she managed to pay her bills on a fixed income amazed and impressed all of us. We speculated that if our mother could sacrifice and pay off her bills with a fixed income, certainly we should be able to manage our finances appropriately. She paid for two burial plots, as well as the opening and closing of the plots. Her receipts and the name of the plots were filed in order. My mother always taught us valuable lessons throughout life, and even through death, she demonstrated to us how finances should be conducted. Mom exclaimed, "It is not how much money you make, but what you do with the money." She always told us to save for a rainy day.

Although my mother never explicitly explained her funeral arrangements with me, she prepared for her funeral and did not want me to worry about her. I realized that God had answered my prayers long ago, and I am grateful that He did. My concern about my mother's wishes concerning her death was already answered. Glory to God!

God, I thank You for answering my heartfelt prayers; you listened and did not reject me. God, I thank You for being a refuge for my mother in death. God, I thank You for allowing the Holy Spirit to be our Comforter. Lord, I praise You for not letting our hearts be consumed with grief. Most importantly, I thank You for giving me a mother who feared and reverenced You. She taught her family morals, respect, love, finances, and about the goodness of the Lord. She blessed our family with her wisdom and insight. She did not compromise her values and always leaned and depended on You. She let us know that little becomes much in the Master's hands. Our mother was a virtuous woman of God who led by example. I am eternally grateful that You allowed her to be in our lives, and I am elated that she introduced us to You.

Gone too Soon

Lord, not again, Lord, not again! It has been eight months since my mother's untimely death, and we are still grieving. It seems like a nightmare all over again. Earnest Virgil East II, passed away on March 27, 2008, at 9 a.m. from three fatal gunshot wounds to the head and back. He was 20 years old.

I returned home from work and entered my bedroom. I noticed my answering machine had eleven recorded messages. I listened to the messages while changing my work clothes. The first message was from my niece, Kimberly. Her soft tone of voice conveyed to me that she was distraught. A homicide detective had contacted her about her son, Earnest, who was allegedly a victim of a violent crime. Apparently, he was shot several times, and they wanted her to come to the hospital and identify the victim. She expressed her concerns and hoped that the victim was not her son, and after she received the devastating news, all she could do was kneel down and pray. The next jarring message was from her husband, Terry, who also sounded devastated. He said that they were at the hospital and that the alleged victim was their son, Earnest, who was comatose and had been placed on life support in the Intensive Care Unit in critical condition. The physician emphasized that if Earnest survived, he would be in a vegetative state. The next message was from my sister, Mary; she was crying.

She sounded overwhelmed and said, "Oh Lord, Berney. This is Mary. Earnest just died!"

I was astonished at the barrage of horrifying messages. I listened carefully to the messages and I could not believe what I heard on the answering machine; it was as if I was in the twilight zone. The jarring messages struck a chord in my heart. So much so, that my heart rate began to accelerate. I tried to remain calm as I immediately picked up the phone to call Kimberly and tell her that I would be arriving at the hospital in approximately 40 minutes. I left a note for my husband, explaining the horrid ordeal. Then I drove to Andre's job and told him the unfortunate news. He was shocked, and his employer allowed him to leave his job early.

We were anxious when we arrived at the hospital and anticipated the worst-case scenario. Our suspicions were validated once we entered the Intensive Care room.

The guard asked everyone for their identification except for me. Then he said, "The family is waiting for your arrival." As I entered the dark room, I noticed the drawn curtains around his bed, and there was an atmosphere of gloom and disheartenment. The tear-jerking incident was calamitous. I tenderly embraced my niece, Kimberly (Earnest's mother) as she devoted all her undivided attention to her son.

Although the phone call from Mary informed me that Earnest was dead, he was actually clinging to life. He was placed on a life support machine. I glanced around the room and noticed the oscilloscope, which displayed his vital signs and central venous pressure. I read the labels on the IV fluids that were infusing into Earnest's lifeless body. I glanced at the patient; it was indeed my great-nephew, whose athletic body was lying comatose in the bed. His head was wrapped with white kerlix dressing, which was saturated with pink tinged secretions. Clear secretions oozed from his eyes, and his nurse wiped the secretions away with tissues that were at his bedside. The endotracheal tube was attached to the respirator that was assisting him to breathe, and a cervical collar was placed around his neck to keep his vertebrae in the neutral position and prevent further injuries from his neck, back, and spine. I touched Earnest's body; he was extremely warm. His nurse placed ice packs on his extremities and removed blankets from his bed to help decrease his temperature.

I communicated with Earnest's nurse, who was on duty when he arrived at the hospital. She said, "Earnest's pupils were dilated at the time of his admission. His EEG confirmed brain stem infarction. You know, he is brain-dead, and the neurologist will perform a second EEG test tomorrow for confirmation." I thanked her for her update on Earnest's condition, and I knew the situation appeared grim. I understood why Mary phoned me and said he was dead, because of the result of the EEG. After the nurse left the room, Kimberly asked me my honest opinion about the situation. I lovingly told her that Earnest was no longer with us. Neurologically, he had no brain function, and the respirator was assisting him to breath. She looked at me apathetically and did not respond. She was overwhelmed and desperate and needed time to absorb what had happened.

The entire horrific scene was breathtaking. Shot twice in the head and once in the back, Earnest had apparently been defenseless against his perpetrators. My thoughts were racing a thousand miles a minute, desperately trying to comprehend who would commit such a brutal act.

This gangster-style execution appeared like something out of the movies. Could this tragedy have occurred because of a gang initiation, or was it his appointed time to die? Earnest was not affiliated with a gang. I know everyone has an appointed time to die, but why this way, Lord? The questions kept surging through my mind. Dreadful emotions welled up inside of me that I never knew existed. The person or persons who had committed the crime neither valued life nor feared God.

This was the fourth occurrence of a homicide in our family due to fatal shootings. Enough is enough! The homicides confirm to me the reality of Satan. His intentions are to kill and destroy humanity by any means necessary, and he is bold about executing assassinations. He does not care whom he uses or exploits to get the job done. The perpetrators who committed these crimes are cold-blooded, heartless murderers. Their hearts are where hatred brews. This heinous crime brought us closer to God, sorrowful, and yet prayerful.

My heart sank when I gazed into the eyes of his mother, who appeared hurt, sorrowful, helpless, and dishearten. I observed her as she gently stroked her son's lifeless body, tears rolling down her cheeks. I wanted desperately to comfort her, but words could not relieve her agony. Our family was deeply saddened and weary. The morbid expressions on all their faces said it all. While some family members stood around the bedside, others sat quietly. I whispered a prayer to the Lord, asking Him to have mercy on us. I asked Him to help us not to faint. *I thought to myself that the devil is a lie! We were going to trust God to see us through this trial.* Christ's strength sustained us through Earnest's death.

Our grief-stricken family needed encouragement, and I told them with conviction that we would get through the ordeal with the help of the Lord! Somehow, they believed me, because their demeanor changed. We resorted to what always seems natural—prayer. We gathered around Earnest's bedside, and each family member took turns praying while seeking guidance from the Lord. Our prayers were to accept God's will, regardless of the outcome. His Word declares that we can "cast your cares on the LORD and he will sustain you; he will never let the righteous fall," (Psalm 55:22) no matter how bleak the situation appears. He's concerned about our problems and makes provision for our needs, and Christ is attentive to our cares.

The next day, May 27, 2008, Earnest Galvin East II died at 9:00 a.m. Kimberly had difficulty accepting the physician's confirmation that Earnest was neurologically brain-dead. Our pastor consoled

Kimberly as he reiterated what the physicians had said, telling her it was time to let Earnest go. As Kimberly cried while the respiratory therapist removed Earnest from the respirator, I recalled John 14:1 says, "Do not let not your heart be troubled." God is with us and He is close to the brokenhearted.

Our family was under tremendous stress, but we persevered to prepare for Earnest's funeral. Kimberly arranged to purchase the plot, programs, and flower arrangements, etc. Although I worked frantically on the funeral arrangements with Kim, the arrangements were becoming cumbersome for her. She felt overwhelmed, so she decided to reschedule the funeral for the following Friday.

The sun shined brilliantly from the sky as the birds chirped a sweet melody, and the leaves on the trees swayed softy. However, we dreaded this day—this was the day of Earnest's funeral. Our family members exited the limousine and lined up two by two as the funeral director led the procession into the sanctuary. It is usually a blessing to enter into the house of the Lord, except for on this sad occasion. Earnest's remains lay in a grey coffin, and he was dressed in a black suit with a red and black tie. He appeared as if he were sleeping, but unfortunately, his life had come to a tragic end. The ushers seated the family in the front pews of the church. We sat quietly, listened to the minister, and were grateful for everyone who participated in the program. Their words of encouragement, songs, and prayers reassured us that God does not make any mistakes. The whole daunting experience made us feel like we were on an emotional roller coaster, but we still felt God's presence and were relieved after we left the funeral.

Experiencing the death of a loved one invokes indescribable emotions. There is finality to death, which many people do not understand. Death has no dominion or power over Christians. Jesus was victorious at the cross, and His atoning blood covered a multitude of sins. Because of His bloodshed, everlasting life is promised to the believer. This promise keeps us hopeful about the demise of our loved ones.

Earnest's death allowed us to evaluate our lives. Our family prayers had contributed a measure of strength, which helped us cope with our grief and emotions. God comforted us during our bereavement as He reaffirmed our faith. Our grief was lessened by His compassion, which helped to mend our fragile hearts. Because of our relationship with God, downcast spirits were lifted and broken heartedness began to dissipate. We relied on Him, and He made provisions for our necessities. We prayed sincerely to God, and He responded with His unmerited favor and love. At our lowest moment, He is at the pinnacle of our grief, and He understands our predicament.

How did we overcome the grief from the death of two of our family members? We inquired of the Lord as we fixed our eyes upon Jesus. We concentrated on Him as our central focal point, drawing immensely from His fountain of living water, which refreshes, cleanses, and satisfies the soul. Despite our tears, anguish, and despair, we obtained God's blessings and favor, and the Holy Spirit enabled us to endure the agony. God assisted us in working through our grief one day at a time. He controls every situation, and we found contentment in Him. Our faith resides in knowing God's sovereignty. We learned to trust Him, walk in faith, and pray for a breakthrough. His love struck a chord in our hearts, and we felt hope at the point of despair. We prayed frequently with family members and friends, as well as privately, prayerfully pursuing God and listening to His voice as He revealed Himself to us.

The sufficiency of God's grace met our spiritual and physical needs. When words failed, God prevailed in our lives, and His spiritual guidelines were explicit in helping us heal, reminding us of His infinite blessings.

How do we overcome the grief stemming from the death of a loved one? Possess the desire to heal and keep the memory of your loved ones in your heart. Pray sincerely, seek God, meditate on His word, and recall the affection He has for you. The righteous have a refuge in Jesus. We know blessed are the dead who die in the Lord from now on. "Yes," says the Spirit, "they will rest from their labor, for their deeds will follow them" (Revelation 14:13).

CHAPTER NINE

Intercessory Prayer

*"I looked for a man among them who would build up the wall
and stand before me in the gap on behalf of the land
so I would not have to destroy it, but I found none."
Ezekiel 22:30*

My nursing assignment entailed caring for an extremely ill patient, and as we conversed, he asked me to pray for him because he wanted to die. Needless to say, I was startled at his request. I couldn't remember the last time I'd seriously engaged in prayer or talked to God, and I recognized that my life wasn't an example of a devout Christian. I knew God, of course, but I wasn't faithfully committed to pray and obey His commandments. I had backslid, and I even doubted that I was in God's will.

My patient was sincere in his request, but at that very moment, I hesitated to respond. Fleeting questions surged through my mind: *If I pray, will God hear me? If He hears me, will He answer my prayer?* My patient needed someone to pray who had great faith and could boldly approach the throne of God, and for this reason, I was reluctant to respond to his request. The desperate gaze in his eyes and the strain in his voice revealed to me the extent of his agony, and I did not want to add to his misery.

Out of compassion, I responded, "God is not ready for you yet."

He said, "I'm tired, and I want to die."

I said, "You need to rest."

I made him as comfortable as I could and then I left the room. I empathized with his situation, because he impressed upon me the importance to communicate with God. He wanted me to pray for God to ease his misery and end his life. His faith revealed to me the essence of a Christian who was not afraid to die. I thought about our conversation a lot, and I began to examine my relationship with God.

Have you ever experienced a predicament in which someone asked you to pray for him or her and you didn't know exactly how to comply? You realized that you were not equipped to intervene in such an emergent situation. This is a very uncomfortable situation to experience, especially when a person sincerely requests prayer and you are unable to grant his or her request.

The conversation with my patient troubled me; therefore, I began to search and examine my faith. Since then, I've drawn closer to the Lord. I've promised Him that I would never refrain from praying for anyone that requested prayer. Fear, guilt, and lack of faith had prevented me from praying for my patient, and my sinful nature prohibited me from seeking God's mercy. As 1 John 1:9 reveals, confession of sins allows God to cleanse us from all unrighteousness. His purification makes our unrighteousness dissipate. My confession would have brought God's forgiveness and blessing. I failed that assignment, but I gained valuable knowledge about myself. My spiritual condition was weak, and my soul was discontent. Most importantly, I had forsaken God. I realized I didn't understand how to intercede on behalf of another person or myself. "Intercession" means "to impinge, entreat, fall upon, intrigue, reach, run."[10] God is searching for intercessors that are bold and confident, willing to pray at any given time—regardless of their surroundings or circumstance. Intercessory prayer grants God's favor; prayerlessness brings God's judgment. Prayerlessness is a disconnection between man and God, a divergence that allows man to maneuver away from Him instead of connecting to Him.

Hebrews 4:16 emphasizes, "Let us then approach the throne of grace with confidence, so that we may receive mercy and find grace to help us in our time of need." Intercessors are bold, and their unrelenting prayers demonstrate confidence and the absence of fear; they respect God's authority and position. Intercessors take a vicarious position to pray with and for individuals in need. Their faith, endurance, and consistent prayer lives exemplify their commitment to God, and their spontaneous and compelling prayers demonstrate their compassion for people. They realize prayer is not a waste of time, but rather time well spent with the Lord. Intercessors learn how to plead, petition, and trust God, striving to close the gap between man and God with an influx of prayers. Their persistent prayers ultimately impress upon the mind of God the need for His assistance. Their prayers are the hedge of protection and a sweet aroma to God's nostrils.

Intercessory prayers are vital to man's existence. When men wholeheartedly pray, they receive God's blessings instead of His curses. The Bible depicts superb illustrations for the necessity of intercessory prayer:

- Job was mindful of his children's inclination to sin, so he prayed for his children in case they sinned against God (Job 1:5).
- The Greek woman born in Syrian Phoenician interceded for her daughter and asked Jesus to cast out the demonic spirit dwelling within her daughter (Mark 7:26).
- Queen Esther's unwavering faith compelled the Jewish people to fast and pray for three days because of a decree made to destroy the Jewish nation. Esther's life was endangered when she approached the king. Nevertheless, she was determined to intercede for the Jews and said, "If I perish, I perish." Queen Esther is the embodiment of a heroine (Esther 4:16).
- All night, troubled Samuel stood in the gap and cried out to the Lord in prayer for Saul, pleading for God not to take away his kingship (1Samuel 15:11).

The Book of Acts is a conceptual framework of God's promise being fulfilled and revealed to the apostles. They received *dunamis* while they were praying because they obeyed Jesus' instructions. Acts 1:8 proclaims, "But you will receive power when the Holy Spirit comes on you; and you will be my witnesses in Jerusalem, and in all Judea and Samaria, and to the ends of the earth." The blessing was two–fold: they received the Holy Spirit and the power to serve as witnesses for the gospel to the world, and they exhibited unification of their hearts and spirits as they prayed. The apostles' prayers echoed throughout Jerusalem, among every tribe, nation, and tongue. Each nationality heard the apostles' prayers in their native language, and the empowerment of the apostles then occurred because of the indwelling of the Holy Spirit, which essentially invoked the apostles' faith and prayers to consummate the establishment of the church.

The ultimate intercessor is King Jesus, who sits at the right hand of the throne of God in heaven, petitioning God on our behalf. John 17:13 enunciates that Jesus interceded in prayer for His disciples and requested that they receive the full measure of His joy and protection from Satan. The disciples needed to be sanctified and set apart for the work of the Lord. Sanctification is the essential requirement to perform God's work, and the disciples were chosen for the assignment. Jesus prayed, not only for the disciples, but also for future believers to become one in Christ Jesus so that the love God has for Jesus could be manifested in them.

These examples illustrate numerous opportunities for people to intervene and pray. Regardless of the opposition, consecrate yourselves to fast and pray for specific reasons. Although the gravity of their problems was overwhelming, they believed, trusted, and followed God's directions. Their prayers and trust unveiled God's blessing for His people. He relieved despair as He showed compassion. They discovered gratification in God's ability to transform their problems into victory and they relished the opportunity to be used by God.

To prevail in intercessory prayer, one must not be fearful, but rather fearless. You must have a personal relationship with God and a heart for people's problems and well-being. The sole purpose of intercessors is to engage in prayer, seek council, instructions, and refuge in God. Intercessors are constantly warring in prayer, impressing upon God the need for His guidance and intervention, as He imputes spiritual discernment for them to distinguish between spiritual and natural occurrences in people's lives. They stand in the gap, lamenting, praying, and pleading for the blood of Jesus to cover circumstances beyond their control. They effectually pray with power, expectation, and assurance, believing God will protect, direct, and rescue people from their dilemmas. Prayers propelled by faith launch us into a heavenly dimension, which subdues the principalities of darkness. This experience stagnates the enemy's power.

I thank God for granting me another opportunity to enter the arena of prayer, believing and trusting Him for revelation and knowledge to intercede for others. Now I understand the significance of engaging in intercessory prayer—it may save someone's life. Essentially, being led by the Spirit and not intimidated by doubt produces an efficacious prayer life. Illustrations of intercessory prayers are found throughout the Bible, to validate the significance of intercessors and how they achieved victorious outcomes through miraculous prayers.

Rise up and Walk!

"Then Peter said, 'Silver and gold I do not have, but what I do have I give you: In the name of Jesus Christ of Nazareth, rise up and walk'" (Acts 3:6 NKJV). Today, people are able to rise up from a deathbed situation and walk in dignity because of faith and prayer. Faith is the conduit used to elicit prayer to manifest God's ability to heal incomprehensible conditions.

A man of faith visited Alice (patient) in the hospital; she was critically ill, mechanically ventilated, and paralyzed. This tall, statuesque man cordially greeted the nurses at the nursing station, and I noticed he was carrying a Bible in his hand as he entered the patient's room and began to pray boldly, with vigor and power. The intensity of the prayer penetrated my ears, and I listened as he prayed with power and conviction.

Although the man prayed in a different language, I felt the surge of the Holy Spirit. The Bible declares, "The Spirit himself testifies with our spirit that we are God's children" (Romans 8:16). As I witnessed him approach the throne of God boldly, this earthen vessel of God had my undivided attention. He prayed with the anointing until I became elated within my spirit; I knew his prayer was not amiss. He interceded in prayer for Alice with authority. His energetic voice was strong, and the longer he prayed, the more powerful he became. God answered his prayer petition, and the evidence was confirmed when Alice critical condition changed to a stable condition. What he sowed in prayer spiritually was manifested by the miraculous physical recuperation of the patient, and she was weaned off the respirator and discharged from the hospital.

James 5:14—15 asks, "Is any one of you sick? He should call the elders of the church to pray over him and anoint him with oil in the name of the Lord. And the prayer offered in faith will make the sick person well; the Lord will raise him up. If he has sinned, he shall be forgiven." Prayer offered in faith heals through the power of God! Whatever sins Alice committed are forgiven through the prayers rendered in faith, which touch God's heart. The grace of God raised

Alice from her sickbed, and she walked into the hospital to thank the nurses for the care she received. We embraced her with love and expressed to her how attractive she looked. This beautiful young woman appeared as though she had never been ill. Alice's breakthrough came after her visitor stood in the gap and rendered a heartfelt intercessory prayer to God.

A Cry for Salvation

"Therefore He is also able to save to the uttermost those who come to God through Him, since He always lives to make intercession for them" (Hebrews 7:25 NKJV). Beverly, a dear friend of mine who is a social worker, called me regarding her client Rochelle, who was very ill. She told me that Rochelle was hospitalized and dying from AIDS, and had requested prayer. Beverly expressed the urgency of this request because they did not know how long Rochelle would live. Beverly gave me the telephone number where Rochelle could be reached and I phoned the hospital to introduce myself to her. I explained to Rochelle the nature of my call, and that I was responding to her prayer request. As we communicated, she spoke in a whisper; her voice sounded very weak. I prayed for Rochelle while we were on the phone, and she provided me with the address of the hospital and her room number.

Several days later, Rochelle was discharged from the hospital and placed under hospice care. Beverly contacted me at the request of Rochelle's family. They wanted me to meet them at the motel where she was residing. When I arrived, Beverly was standing outside waiting for me and told me Rochelle was dying. We knocked on the door and Rochelle's ex-husband ushered us into the room where she was lying in the bed with her eyes closed. We observed Rochelle's daughter and friend who were both vigilant at her bedside.

As I entered, I felt a sense of sadness and gloom, which engulfed the entire room. I approached the ill woman and spoke softly to her, and as I told her my name, she opened her eyes and smiled. She appeared very weak and emaciated. I gathered everyone around her bed for prayer, then asked Rochelle's permission to anoint her head with oil. She agreed, and I proceeded to anoint everyone who was present around her bed—except her daughter's girlfriend, who refused to be anointed because of her faith. I prayed as the family quietly wiped away the tears from their eyes. Although her eyes were closed, she appeared to be at peace. When I finished praying, the family thanked us for coming, and escorted Beverly and me to the door. Later that afternoon, I received a phone call notifying me that Rochelle had died. I do not believe she feared death, because she sought the Lord and accepted God as her personal Savior.

The prayer rendered in faith was to strengthen her family during their time of sorrow, as well as reassure her that death is not the end. Eternal life and peace are promises from Almighty God for all believers. Even though she walked through the valley of the shadow of death, she feared no evil because God was with her (see Psalm 23:4). His rod and staff are used as instruments of comfort for those whose hearts are broken—especially for the loved ones who are grieving from the loss. We thanked God for Rochelle's life.

"The fruit of the righteous is a tree of life, and he who wins souls is wise" (Proverbs 11:30). This soul was saved because of her faith to seek and accept God into her life. God possesses the ability to save people who believe in His darling Son, Jesus Christ. He comforts the brokenhearted. Rochelle heard the gospel and believed in prayer; therefore, she shall receive everlasting life. Thank God for the woman or man who is able to step in the gap and lead sinners to Christ for God to receive the glory.

God's Goodness

"For the LORD *is* good; His mercy *is* everlasting, And His truth endures to all generations" (Psalm 100:5 NKJV). One Sunday afternoon, I received a phone call from my friend Alicia, who expressed concerns regarding her hospitalized cousin. She explained that John and his roommate were requesting prayer, and she asked if I would pray with them. I assured her I would visit them Monday afternoon. I asked her if John was saved, and she said that John knew the Lord—but that he had backslid and she wasn't sure about his roommate's salvation. She explained how gracious God had been to John. He had previously been shot seven times and recovered from that crises.

I responded in amazement, "What a testimony!" I then asked her for his room number, and she told me that he was on the seventh floor, Room 701.

I repeated what Alicia said. "You said that John had previously been shot seven times and that his room is located on the seventh floor, Room 701."

She responded, "Yes."

I explained, "The number seven is completion. It's time for the prodigal son to return to God. He is a testament of the dispensation of

God's grace and mercy, which has kept him alive, and he can testify about the goodness of the Lord. Tell John I'll come to visit them Monday afternoon."

The next day, I returned to work and experienced a grueling assignment. When I completed my shift I was exhausted, but I remembered the commitment I had made to John, so I went to my locker to retrieve the Bibles I'd brought to the hospital for John and his roommate. The church had donated the Bibles to assist in the ministry for lost souls. As I walked slowly down the long corridor, I whispered a prayer to God as I embraced the Bibles close to my heart, saying, "God, tell me what to say to these men." I rode the elevator to the seventh floor, then got off and entered a quiet room. I glanced at the man in the first bed and said, "Are you John?"

He said, "No, John is in the next bed."

I was still embracing the Bibles as I slowly walked over to the next bed and peaked around the curtains, then our eyes met and he enthusiastically said, "I know who you are you are—Alicia's friend!"

I smiled as I introduced myself to him. Then I said, "Yes, Alicia sent me. I am here because you requested prayer." He nodded his head enthusiastically up and down, indicating yes.

I continued to embrace the Bibles, and as I was looking at him I said, "God is good."

He said, "I have that Scripture on my cell phone!" As he sat up in bed, he grew even more excited, and his eyes sparkled as he asked me to pass him the cell phone on the windowsill. He then turned it on and passed it back to me, and I read the Scripture displayed on his cell phone: "God is good."

John and I smiled at each other, and suddenly I was in the Spirit and felt rejuvenated. I started elaborating on the Word of God, and John listened carefully. It was as though we had known each other all of our lives. John was ill, and he requested me to pray for his healing.

I responded by saying, "God is in the blessing business, and He is able to heal." John's roommate was eavesdropping on our conversation, so I pulled back the curtains and we introduced ourselves to each other. He told me his name was Ariel, and I inscribed his name in the Bible and passed it to him. He could hardly compose himself. The expression on his face indicated that he was deeply touched and appreciated the gift.

He said, "Thank you."

It was evident he wanted to cry, because of the tears that filled his eyes. I began to minister to Ariel.

I said, "Everything you need is in the Bible." As I flipped through the pages of the Bible, I showed him the concordance, the cross-references, and the list of the books of the Bible. I then discussed with him how to search for Scriptures that pertain to circumstances occurring in his life. When you want to read about love, research the word "love" in the concordance, and it will refer you to specific Scriptures, chapters, and verses.

He listened attentively to everything I said, then called someone on the phone and told him or her that a woman had given him a Bible. This was significant because he had never before possessed one. As he was conversing on the phone, I walked back to John's bedside.

John whispered to me, "You blessed him with that Bible, and he needs your prayers because he's paralyzed." John's compelling statement aroused within me an urgent need to stay longer than I had anticipated, to witness to them.

After Ariel finished his conversation on the phone, we continued to fellowship with one another. I adamantly emphasized God as a healer, and His sovereignty. I prayed with John and Ariel, and they thanked me for visiting and praying with them.

James 4:2 asserts, "You do not have, because you do not ask God." John and Ariel asked for prayer, and God responded favorably to their needs. He fulfilled their desires because they asked with the right motive. John and Ariel's requests exhibited their faith. They believed God would send someone to pray for them—which He did—and the jovial experience we encountered with prayer left a lasting impression.

God used me to be a blessing to John and Ariel, granting me the courage to pray with them and for them. Because of their faith, they became recipients of God's blessing. Prayer accompanies faith, and prayerfulness reconnects man to God. This incident led to the revelation of God's goodness and essentially to renewed hope. God answered my prayer and gave me words of encouragement for John and Ariel. Essentially, efficient witnessing transpires from the endowment of the Holy Spirit and God's grace. When I spoke the words "God is good," the Lord confirmed it on John's cell phone. This illustrates how God's goodness underscores the essence of His divinity and His goodness is extended to the believer.

Dropped Charges

While we were in church one Sunday, my sister in Christ asked to speak with me privately. She looked troubled and appeared to be in distress, and she asked me to pray for her son who was incarcerated and facing a prison term. I listened as she explained the trials she was enduring in her life. When she finished, my response to her was, "Have you prayed about the situation? What did the Lord say?"

She held her head down, appearing perplexed. She did not respond to my questions, and it was obvious she was overwhelmed. The Bible proclaims, "When you are in trouble, pray" (James 5:13). I prayerfully interceded for God to change the heart of the district attorney and to avert a prison sentence. After we prayed, we embraced one another, and I reminded her that I would continue to pray for her and her family.

Several Sundays passed, and I missed her presence in church. Concerned about her psychological well-being, I phoned her at home. During our conversation, she explained to me that her mother was ill and that she worked at night, which made it difficult for her to attend church on Sundays. We prayed together on the phone, and I told her she could call me any time to pray. The following week, I saw her in the grocery store, and she told me her son had been released from jail. The district attorney had dismissed the charges.

I said, "Tell Glen to come to church on Sunday and praise God for granting him favor—but the next time he violates the law, he might not receive God's grace or mercy."

God's unmerited favor changed the course of this man's life and the heart of the district attorney. He turned the situation around for

His advantage to receive glory and provided Glen with another opportunity to repent and change his lifestyle.

"Because of the LORD'S great love we are not consumed, for his compassions never fail. They are new every morning" (Lamentations 3:22—23). God loves the sinner, but He hates the sin. He sympathizes with our needs and abstains from destroying us in our wickedness. Displaying immoral conduct is a stench to His nostrils and a defilement of the Holy Spirit that resides within us. God cleanses us with His Word and the blood of Jesus, permitting us to have a right relationship with Him. As such, we should refrain from taking God's mercy for granted. Because of His compassion, mercy, and faithfulness, we must appreciate the daily blessings that He bestows upon us. His mercy permits us to persevere through trials prayerfully.

Can you give me a ride home?

It was a beautiful afternoon, and each classmate eagerly participated in the Bible Study Fellowship (BSF) group discussion. Our study group engaged in an exhilarating dialogue as we discussed our interpretation of the Scriptures. After our group discussion adjourned, we went into the chapel to listen to the overview of the biblical discourse. I listened attentively to the lecturer as she imparted her insights on the lesson, and I was astonished by the wisdom I received from reading the lecture notes.

After our Bible study class was dismissed my prayer partner, Karen, asked me for a ride home. I said, "Sure, I'll take you home."

A few moments later, Amira asked me for a ride home. I looked in amazement and said, "What kind of Christian would I be if I couldn't give you a ride home?"

We gathered our Bibles and biblical assignments and briskly walked to my car. After we were inside, I proceeded to drive down the street, when Amira spoke softly and requested prayer for her son who was incarcerated. She informed us that he was dealing with some anger issues and needed prayer. As I felt the agony and disappointment in her voice while she conveyed to us what was occurring in his life, I suddenly parked the car near some apartments located down the street from the church. I realized God had orchestrated this event and it was not a coincidence that both of these women needed a ride home; it was a Divine appointment to engage in intercessory prayer for Amira and her son.

As we touched hands and agreed about the prayer petition, we immediately began praying in the Spirit. We continued to pray boldly and sincerely until the windows in my car were fogged over. We were so entrenched in prayer that I had forgotten to turn off the engine to the car and had left my headlights on. Thank God the car was in park!

We continued to pray until we felt that the stronghold was broken. Finally, we were released from the Holy Spirit, and my spirit felt lifted. I felt as though I could run to the church, fall down on my knees at the altar, and worship the Lord. The psalmist proclaims, "Oh, magnify the LORD with me, And let us exalt His name together. I sought the LORD, and He heard me, And delivered me from all my fears" (Psalm 34:3—4 NKJV). Magnifying the Lord and exalting His name together causes miraculous things to occur. The spirit of fear is destroyed, the spirit of despair is torn down, and the spirit of disappointment is annihilated. Glory to His name! Satan is defeated when he attempts to make you think that you are the only one who has problems with your children. Intercessory prayer is vital component to combat spiritual wickedness, and as a result, it reveals God's discernment concerning the situation. Prayer had eased Amira's mind and decreased her anxiety, and we praised and thanked God for the opportunity to intercede for her son.

"For where two or three are gathered together in My name, I am there in the midst of them" (Matthew 18:20 NKJV). We prayed in Jesus' name, and He became involved; He positioned Himself to be in the midst of our worship and praise. Jesus is mindful of our struggles and concerned about our problems, and He turned the situation around to receive glory.

When we attended BSF the following Monday night, Amira testified about her son's release from jail the same night that we'd interceded in prayer. Her testimony blessed me, and I learned a valuable lesson about intercessory prayer. An intercessor's spontaneous prayer draws on God's power, instead of concentrating on the problem. Saints are hurting and have issues, baggage, and heavy burdens—but all these burdens are ultimately lifted by the sincerity of our prayers. God bears the brunt of our problems in order to relieve frustration that saddens us because of failed expectations. Romans 12:12—13 encourages us to, "Be joyful in hope, patient in affliction, faithful in prayer. Share with God's people who are in need."

Intercessory prayer activates faith to obtain grace, which permits our entrance into the throne room of God. Prayer is the remedy to restore hope, combat afflictions, and strengthen our faith. Prayer counteracts troubled spirits and is the gateway to receive a spiritual endowment of God's power.

Vigilant Son

"And a voice from heaven said, 'This is my Son, whom I love; with him I am well pleased'" (Matthew 3:17). The relationship between a father and son is endearing, just like the relationship between a mother and son. Parents usually desire the best for their children and want them to be people they can be proud of, who demonstrate maturity by making the right decisions in life at the appropriate times. Parents esteem children who are obedient and listen to parental instructions without rebelling against their advice. They adore children who honor and respect them, not because they are their parents, but out of admiration for who they represent, as well as their morals, integrity, and character.

Jesus, the Son of God, respected His Father and had a spiritual relationship with Him. Jesus was obedient until death. His purpose was to save humanity, and He did not argue with His Father about His predicament; instead, He died willingly on the cross to save sinners and to glorify God. Jesus continually sought God for explicit directions, comfort, and encouragement. He prayed consistently to His Father and claimed, "I and the Father are one" (John 10:30). The triune God glanced down from His throne room through the heavenly firmaments upon earth and declared, "You are my Son, whom I love; with you I am well pleased" (Luke 3:22). God identified his relationship with Jesus, His love for His son, and His adoration for

Him. God was ecstatic about Jesus' Divine ability to save humanity, an expression that all parents desire to proclaim about their own sons: that they are respectful, obedient, and pleasing in their sight.

Scripture explicitly says, "Children, obey your parents in the Lord, for this is right. "Honor your father and mother,"— which is the first commandment with a promise —"that it may go well with you and that you may enjoy long life on the earth" (Ephesians 6:1–3). Longevity of life is a promise from God that is obtained by demonstrating respect and honoring our parents, irrespective of what their demeanors may be. This behavior is right in the sight of the Lord. The promise from God is longevity and favor because we have heeded the Word of God. Children who are disobedient, defiant, and rebellious against their parents are committing sin against a holy God. Instead of receiving His blessings, they will receive God's judgment.

While I was working in the critical care unit, I had the opportunity to observe a son who honored his mother. He caught my attention when he walked into the unit with a Bible in his hand. He came to visit his mother, who was on a life-support system. As he sat down in a chair by her bedside and began to read Scriptures to her, I watched him intervene with her as he gently stroked her forehead and kissed her cheek. Although she was sedated and unable to respond, he continued to read passages faithfully to his mother. I thought to myself, *What a dedicated son he is, very attentive and thoughtful.*

I entered the room and introduced myself to him. I asked him if he had any questions regarding his mother's care. He began to converse with me and asked several questions about his mother's progress. After our conversation about her illness, I asked him if he prayed for his mother. His response was no. He told me that she was a prayerful woman. I then encouraged him to pray for her recovery and anoint her head with oil. He was compliant and began to pray for his mother, and he anointed her head with oil as he prayed a fervent prayer for her healing. As she heard him praying, her eyes opened, and she made eye contact with him, tears rolled down her cheeks as he continued to pray for her recovery. I felt the presence of the Lord as he gently wiped away her tears, demonstrating the love they had for one another. Apparently they had a unique relationship, by his mother's reaction to his touch. She tried to speak, and although her words were not audible, she expressed with her mouth, "I love you."

"Honor thy mother and father so it will go well with you." God blessed this young man who honored his mother and prayed for her recovery. His spiritual Father and mother were pleased with him. Being obedient to the Word of God blesses the believer, and God's blessing often allows us to bless people who are in need and unable to pray for themselves. Her son's obedience to God gave him favor for his mother to recuperate from her illness. The healing virtue of God was evident when she recovered—not because of modern medicine—but because of her son's faith in the power of prayer. His ability to stand in the gap and intercede for his mother occurred because of his faith, and his mother can truly say, "This is my son, with whom I am well pleased."

God Gave Me a Church

"But when you pray, go into your room, close the door and pray to your Father, who is unseen. Then your Father, who sees what is done in secret, will reward you" (Matthew 6:6). Our house was unoccupied, so we placed an ad in the paper for a prospective renter. Unbeknownst to my husband, I went into my secret closet and prayed to the Lord to send us a tenant who was saved and who loved the Lord. I wanted the transaction to be a stress free event without landlord or tenant issues.

We meticulously cleaned our home and contacted painters to paint the walls for a new occupant. I then prepared the applications for prospective tenants to complete and mail to our residence, and we began the tedious process of interviewing and screening the applicants. My husband was excited after he interviewed a prospective tenant whom he felt met the qualifications for the rental. This young woman was cordial, married, and had a good credit history. After viewing the home with my husband, she said she liked it, so we scheduled an appointment for the couple to view the home at a future date. However, the Holy Spirit revealed to me that this couple wouldn't be the occupants of our home.

I never discussed my concerns with my husband, though, because I didn't want to disappoint him. He had worked diligently to prepare the house for the prospective tenants. When the young couple arrived to view our home, they explained their concerns about their ability to pay rent. We then encouraged them to discuss the situation among themselves and contact us later with their decision. In the meantime, we continued to solicit tenants.

One day while the painters were painting, more prospective tenants came by to view the house. They inquired whom the property owners were and requested an application. We were not present at the time, but they toured the home while the painters were present, and then asked them to remove the "For Rent" sign. The painters contacted my husband and told him about the prospective tenants who were interested in renting our home. Excited, my husband explained the situation to me.

"Honey, you won't believe this! Several people came to view the house while the painters were there and told them they want to rent it."

As I listened, I heard the enthusiasm in my husband's voice. He said, "These people are clergy from a church, and they want to rent the house for their pastor. While they were inspecting the house, they removed the sign from the window."

They were definitely claiming things "that are not as though they were" (Romans 4:17). When Ronald finished speaking, I expressed my concerns to him.

I said, "They should not have been on the premises without our permission or presence."

I then realized what he had said: *They were from a church and they wanted to rent the house for their pastor.* We scheduled an appointment with the executives of their church, and we agreed to rent the property to them. We reviewed the contract with them, and all parties agreed and signed the contract.

After they left the meeting, I told Ronald about my prayer, that I had prayed for God to send us a saved person who loved the Lord—and to my amazement, He'd responded favorably by blessing us with the Phillips Temple Christian Methodist Episcopal Church and their pastor. What an awesome God we serve! God hears prayers prayed in secrecy, and He honored my request. He definitely rewards those who diligently seek Him.

Adamant Prayers, Radical Results

Who can pray, that God will hear? Who can pray, and God will respond? Audacious men and women of faith who seek God with sincerity of heart can. God is attentive to the needs of His people, patiently waiting for someone, somewhere to stand in the gap and declare, "Here am I, Lord; send me" (Isaiah 6:8). Christian's, desire to participate in intercessory prayer, because it bridges many people's lives back to God. Your prayer life is enriched because of your ability to be transparent and used by God.

CHAPTER TEN

Denied Prayer Requests

"When you spread out your hands in prayer, I will hide my eyes from you; even if you offer many prayers, I will not listen. Your hands are full of blood; wash and make yourselves clean."
Isaiah 1:15

I have cried all day and throughout the night. My tears have dried up like a stream in the desert from the scorching sun. God, can You hear me? Please answer my prayer! I look around anxiously, and I do not see anyone. Oh God, I need to feel Your presence, because I remain in despair. Merciful God, do you care? Please respond quickly as You listen attentively to my prayer.

Have you ever prayed and not received a response from God? On the other hand, have you ever prayed and your petition was denied? Many people believe that God answers all prayers favorably, but there is no validity to this pragmatic concept. This misconception derives from people who are oblivious to God's essence. God does not answer every prayer according to our expectations. Instead, He analyzes our prayers in several ways. He either grants the request or denies the petition, and He can also provide a waiting period or reject supplications that are prayed amiss.

Job says, "I cry out to you, O God, but you do not answer; I stand up, but you merely look at me" (Job 30:20). Why did Job's prayer fall on deaf ears? God tested Job's faith, and untested faith is misguided hope. God was perfecting Job's faith through hardship, and denied prayer requests dishearten many people who usually emphasize: (1) Prayer did not work for me, or (2) I have prayed, and God did not answer my prayer. These statements are a cop out. Now, let's be honest. Many people desire a microwave fix for an avalanche of problems. Ask yourself if you are praying in the will of God. Are you obedient to His Word? Are you saved? Does your conduct and character reflect God's image? God says to the wicked, "What right have you to recite my laws or take my covenant on your lips? You hate my instruction and cast my words behind you" (Psalm 50:16).

Job, a righteous man, was acquainted with God, and he teaches us a valuable lesson about prayer. He said, "Though he slay me, yet will I hope in him" (Job 13:15). While he was enduring persecution, Job realized God had his best interest at heart. Job's faith was not contingent on his wealth, but rather on his relationship with God. His wife suggested to Job that he curse God and die, but he did not curse God—he blessed Him. Job maintained his integrity and continued to be prayerful as he faced opposition. He never jeopardized his prayer life, even though he did not understand God's response. He was compelled to pray and search for revelation from God.

Why is prayer appalling to some people and compelling to others? God does not answer prayers as we anticipate or to our specifications. He is not a bellhop, a genie in a bottle, or Santa Claus. He does not operate in that capacity. Instead, He fulfills our necessities and does not handle prayers with preferential treatment—especially if we are out of His will. We cannot coerce God! He operates according to His holy attributes executing righteous judgment.

An exemplary example of an unfavorable request is illustrated in 2 Samuel 12:15-18. King David fasted 7 days and prayed for his son's healing, but his prayers did not appease God. God denied David's prayer request because of his premeditated murder scheme to kill Uriah. Saved David reverted to sinful behavior, and God executed judgment for David's heinous crime: his innocent son died because of David's sexual promiscuity. Rejected prayers tainted with bloodshed are an abomination to God. Be mindful to approach God with humility and a heart of repentance.

Moses was a chosen prophet whose prayers God rejected. Moses appealed to God to "let me go over and see the good land beyond the Jordan—that fine hill country and Lebanon" (Deuteronomy 3:25). God rejected Moses' plea to cross over to the Promised Land. "But, because of you the LORD was angry with me and would not listen to me. 'That is enough,' the LORD said. 'Do not speak to me anymore about this matter'" (Deuteronomy 3:26). Disobedience brings God's judgment, and He does not listen to excuses. God is not impressed with our emotions; He perceives the intention of our hearts.

If God answered every petition favorably, would we exclusively serve God? Absolutely not! People are usually ungrateful when they receive everything they desire. They become conceited, spoiled, self-righteous individuals who are unappreciative of their blessings. God is just, and He does not operate according to our emotional states. What makes you think you deserve God's blessings when you operate contrary to His commandments? When you hear the gospel and think it is not applicable to your life, you are guilty of omission and commission. "If anyone turns a deaf ear to the law, even his prayers are detestable" (Proverbs 28:9). Your prayers are offensive and repulsive in the sight of the Lord. Indignant behavior displayed toward God is detrimental to your well-being, and you miss your opportunity to be blessed, prosperous, and cheerful. Your superior attitude displeases God, and He will not be mocked! It's impractical to think that God owes us anything; He blesses us because of His abundant mercy and grace. God is our Spiritual Father, and His wisdom supersedes our fleshly desires.

We must continuously examine ourselves and search our hearts thoroughly. Ask yourself if you are a murderer, liar, theft, con artist, atheist, infidel, or a person who deliberately indulges in evil deeds. Paul proclaims, "Be wise about what is good and innocent about what is evil" (Romans 16:19). Are you a proud, arrogant individual who calls on the Lord only when an emergent need arises—and when the need is not urgent, you cease to pray? Perhaps you wonder why God did not respond appropriately as you requested. When you pray, do you lack the faith that causes God to intervene or motivate Him to listen? God mandated prayer, and we must be serious about how we approach Him. Selfishness, sinful hearts, unforgiveness, and anger hinder God's response to our prayers, but yielding to the Holy Spirit blesses our souls to maintain righteous conduct.

God refuses to hear prayers from people who cherish sin in their hearts (Psalm 66:18). Contentious thoughts are a prelude to sinful actions. We must avoid ungodly behavior. Men who do not fear or reverence God have ineffective prayer lives, and the prayers of wicked men condemn them (Psalm 109:7). God does not answer impenitent prayers. People who do not fear God pray with ill-gained intent. God refuses to listen to ungodly requests with vanity, which must not be construed as effectual prayer streaming from the hearts of Godly men who reverence God.

Do Christians stop praying because our prayer petitions are denied? Heaven forbid! We must be cautious of our motives and pray with sincerity. We are not constrained by guilt. Rather, we pray with grateful hearts consecrated unto the Lord.

King David grieved over his son's death, but he never lost his faith or praise. He continued to be prayerful and to fellowship with God. Saints understand that God has their best interests at heart, and they pray according to His will. He will not permit them to succumb to detriment. Prayerfulness exhibits godliness, and Christians who are rooted and grounded in Christ are connected to God through their prayer lives. Never cease to pray, even when your prayers are denied.

A persistent prayer life is full of rejections and approvals from God. Just like when working with a loan officer who accepts some applications and rejects others, you continue to submit your application until it is approved. Therefore, continue to submit your prayer request to God. Prayerful spirits are the magnets that draw us closer to God; they hinge upon the Christ atonement and our faith. Christians believe supernatural events can transpire with an omnipotent God. Prayer becomes the anchor in our lives and a pillar of strength; it flows from our hearts like the blood that flows throughout our veins. Prayer is a vital component of our Christianity; it is a pathway to healing, maturity, and wisdom. This spiritual encounter draws us closer to God.

The efficacy of our prayers relies on our faith. Do you possess mountain-moving faith—faith that causes healing, deliverance, ability to cast out demons, and provides liberation of freedom? Or does God look at you and say, "Oh, ye of little faith?" Our faith is the epitome of our heartfelt prayers. God will challenge and test us to determine if we will prevail in prayer. There are times when our spirits are willing to pray, but our flesh becomes vulnerable. Regardless of how we feel, though, we must remain prayerful. Our Advocate and High Priest is Christ Jesus, Who continually makes intercessions on behalf of the saints, and so should we.

We possess the ability to pray in Jesus' name, trusting God and believing unconditionally that He listens to our supplications. Our objective is to be steadfast, displaying an unmovable force that never wavers from our position as we wait patiently for God's response. "But let patience have *its* perfect work, that you may be perfect and complete, lacking nothing" (James 1:4 NKJV). Patience is a disciplined behavior that demonstrates self-control during provocative situations. You have contentment in the midst of turmoil, because of the Holy Spirit that dwells within you; this demonstrates to God your ability to remain calm during misfortune, while you withstand pressure. Prayer invigorates us with the stamina to continue praying while relying on God to assist us through the disconcerting situations. Our temperament does not change, and we do not become impatient and take matters into our own hands. Praying takes perseverance and patience. Despite our hardships, we continue to pray for a positive outcome, believing and affirming that everything will work out for the good of those who love the Lord (Romans 8:28). Praying fills the void of helplessness as it restores hope, and removes vices that hinder our ability to communicate with God. We believe God can change predicaments and situations. Therefore, we press towards a higher calling in Christ—a calling for a commitment to pray to overcome our problems leaving past failures in the past.

There is something mystical about prayer. You can pray, but God does not have to respond. And when God responds to prayers, it's not according to our timing. His response can be instantaneous or take months, years, or a lifetime. Regardless of whether God answers your prayers or rejects them, continue to pray faithfully. Your blessings will eventually outweigh the prayers that were denied. I encourage you to pray with a grateful heart. Prayer never fails, but we fail to realize that God can bless or curse anyone or anything that He desires. Adhere to God's word and draw on His sustenance and power. Unyielding prayers illustrate our commitment to God and our sincerity about prayer. Remember, there are no valid excuses to stop praying. However, there are numerous reasons to continue to pray. Prayerfulness is our window of opportunity to pursue God wholeheartedly.

God has not answered all of my prayers, yet I maintain a prayerful mentality. Why? He exceeds my expectations. Therefore, I know He is able to do exceedingly more than I can imagine. I trust God, and I believe His word is true. The evidence is written in the Bible, which reveals His will for my life. Not my will, Lord, but let Thy will be done. He plans to perfect the good work He established within me while He blesses me with a prosperous future: to be the head and not the tail, to be the lender and not the borrower, and to live a victorious life until the coming of Jesus Christ. I must maintain my faith and integrity, while displaying my commitment to remain prayerful.

To me, prayer is like fertilizer: you cannot visualize its effects until you've used the product. It takes time for the fertilizer to penetrate the soil, and using it as instructed produces good results. Pray frequently with sincerity; acknowledge that you don't know which prayers God will answer. But eventually you will see the fruition of your labor. God does answer prayers. Keep a journal to remind you of the prayers God has answered and describe how He responded. The prayer seed sown in faith enables God to reap the harvest because it's sown in fertile soil and the prayers God answers give us the assurance of His compassion.

God has not denied my entire prayer requests. He has answered my questions about ministry and my spiritual gifts, He has guided me through the trials to test my commitment and faith, and He has blessed me with the discernment to differentiate friends from enemies. I cannot refrain from praying to allow the enemy to steal my joy or my blessings. Prayerfulness is embedded within my heart. I need God's wisdom, guidance, comfort, blessings, and strength—I need God!

Do you need Him to navigate your life? Engage in a dialogue with Him by praying. We need to be prayerful about every situation we encounter. Empowerment comes from a consistent prayer life that acknowledges God. Unselfish acts of prayer compel God to intervene on our behalves. Make a commitment to wait on God's response to your prayers, and accept His answer without resentment. Not every prayer will be answered according to your specification, but denied requests are often beneficial to our well-beings. If God granted every prayer request, it would bring detriment into our lives. Be conscientious of your prayer life and make sure you're prepared to receive God's answer to your prayers.

Be mindful that while you're praying, God is working on your character, conduct, and faith, and bringing you to a level of maturity. Wait on the Lord! Do not take matters into your own hands, because it will complicate the situation. Trust God and praise Him until He turns the situation around. Your praise causes Him to grant you favor in the situation. We do not control our destiny, God does. Let God direct your path to righteousness. Continue to pray with confidence without wavering in your faith. "Ask God for the words of your mouth and the meditation of your heart to be pleasing in His sight" (Psalm 19:14).

CHAPTER ELEVEN

The Prayerful Church

> "And I tell you that you are Peter, and on this rock I will build my church, and the gates of Hades will not overcome it."
> Matthew 16:18

House of Prayer

The church is built on the foundation of the apostle, prophets, and blood of Jesus. God's church is constructed upon the salvation work at the cross. Jesus built His church on Petra, the rock of truth. This rock is a firm foundation; it is solid, sturdy, and dependable, incapable of destruction. Christians' faith in Jesus joins us together to become a holy temple, a dwelling place where the Holy Spirit can reside. Jesus is the precious cornerstone and the plumb line that establishes justice and righteousness in the house of God. Upon this foundation, hell cannot—and is incapable of—sabotaging or overpowering God's sanctuary, which is a refuge of hope.

Jesus said, "This is the house of prayer." Prayer is potent, powerful, and effective, the essential weapon needed to cast out evil spirits. Jesus imputed a spirit of prayer into the house of God. Even though Christians can always resort to prayer as a powerful weapon, it is often neglected because we become preoccupied with the function of church auxiliaries, gossip, and complacency. We must combat these demonic forces through corporate prayer. Every time the serpent raises his head to strike us with his venom, we must plead the blood and remain prayerful. We must impinge upon the heart of God the urgency to tear down strongholds that exist in the church. Do not take prayer for granted; instead, be sincere and vigilant concerning prayer to combat demonic forces.

Warfare in Church

What will you do when you experience trouble in the house of God? When vicious insults are intentionally snarled at you and you are criticized for your performance? How do you combat argumenttative spirits that continue to operate in wrongness? How do you correct ornery church members who will neither speak to one another, nor participate in church functions, or saints who are unwilling to work with certain people in the congregation? How do you collaborate with church members who do not believe in tithing? How do you correct fornication, homosexuality, adultery, and schism in the house of God? How do you prevent carnality from infiltrating the house of God and becoming complacent in your stance against fleshly desires? How do you rebuke a deceitful preacher?

"Judgment begins with the family of God; and if it begins with us, what will the outcome be for those who do not obey the gospel of God? And if it is hard for the righteous to be saved, what will become of the ungodly and the sinner?" (1 Peter 4:17—18). God will judge Christians! Ungodly character and behavior is unacceptable in the house of God. I agree with the adage that we cannot be so heavenly bound that we aren't any earthly good. We cannot pretend to be holy and then live ungodly lives that aren't profitable for anyone. We are without excuse because of the preaching, edification, exhortation, and prophetic Word we hear preached on Sunday morning and at Bible Study. Living an unholy life is detestable in the sight of God. He does not dwell in an unclean temple, nor should He. He is a Holy God! He cannot inhabit the praises of His people when their hearts are distant from Him. Unclean hands and contaminated hearts grieve the Lord, and judgment starts with Christians because we are the Body of Christ.

Failure to exhibit holiness in a precarious society jeopardizes our credibility and obscures our commitment to God. He is no longer LORD, because we prevent Him from reigning completely in our hearts or have full range in our lives. He is no longer Master, because we do not obey His will or precepts. This is detrimental to the saints of God because these blemishes taint our hearts, defame our character, and immobilize us from productivity. God instructs His people to obey His commands, love Him, refrain from evil, do good, and exhibit love to one another while being committed to prayer. Failure to obey God's commandments will lead to His wrath. The judgment for sin is death, and the verdict for repentance is forgiveness.

When sin enters the church, it brings discord and disharmony. Instead of leading people to Christ, they are led astray because of our inappropriate conduct. Cantankerous spirits display whoredom, greed, chaos, and gossip—none of which are from God—and these unclean spirits must be rebuked. These people have their own agenda and display demonic spirits of the antichrist; they are negligent in their motives, judgments, thoughts, and deeds. Test the spirit to ascertain if it is truly from God; behavior that does not exemplify the Spirit of

God represents the spirit of the antichrist. This is evident when people refrain from displaying the fruits of the spirit—no fruition, no growth. Ask yourselves, is your church membership growing or dwindling? Christians are held accountable to attain a higher standard in the Lord. We are led by the Holy Spirit and not by man or by our emotions.

Individuals who do not listen to the word of truth are walking in error, so avoid disgruntled people who bring strife among their spiritual brethren. James 3:16 declares, "For where you have envy and selfish ambition, there you find disorder and every evil practice." Evil work is the work of the antichrist. "Strife" is vigorous or bitter conflict, discord or antagonism capable of dividing the church.[11] Evil works are the devil's domain. This dangerous territory allows Satan to run rampant. Satan's tactics are capable of causing strife, confusion, and discord in the church, and observant saints extinguish this vile spirit quickly when it appears in the house of the Lord.

Avoid strife by listening attentively prior to engaging in futile conversation. When the conversation does not instruct or benefit the Body of Christ, then it is idle conversation or gossip. Combat confusion with pleasant words. Corrupt communication should not proceed out of a Christian's mouth, and negative comments are not beneficial to anyone. By exhibiting self-control, you can refrain from commenting on negative conversation. Do not add fuel to the fire! God holds you accountable for bridling your tongue. Counterattack these offenses with prayer and allow the grace of God to intervene. Be a beacon of light and speak the truth; be a blessing to someone instead of a curse. Speak words of wisdom and encourage people who are discouraged. Give people hope when they feel depressed. Your godly behavior demonstrates your love for Christ, and this approach edifies the Body of Christ by allowing you to rebuke and correct gossip. The grace of God will permit people to hear His Words and reject ungodly conversation. A man of God discerns these divisive tactics.

Don't forget: judgment begins at the house of God. "Make every effort to live in peace with all men and to be holy; without holiness, no one will see the Lord" (Hebrews 12:14). Evaluate whether or not the person causing the strife is you. If it is, then correct your behavior, operate in a spiritual mode contrary to the saints who are disobedient, and emulate God's character and will, proclaiming to a perishing world that holiness is right.

Power of Corporate Prayer

When saints are busy tearing down one another, they miss the opportunity to effectively witness to lost souls. In addition, they fall short in building up the Body of Christ. The objective of corporate prayer is to seek God's vision and purpose for the church. Corporate prayer is necessary to build unity and increase faith, as well as to promote love and unification of hearts. These vital components assist saints in overcoming the obstacles that hinder our progress in advancing God's kingdom. Members who actively pray illustrate spiritual harmony within the church.

The Early Church Prayer

The early church demonstrated compassion for their brethren by engaging in prayer. Peter and John are exemplary examples of encouraging corporate prayer. Accused of proclaiming the resurrection of Jesus of Nazareth and His power to heal a crippled man, they were incarcerated, questioned by the Jewish council, and forbidden to teach or speak about Jesus. Acts 4:23 exclaims that on their release, Peter and John went back to their own people and reported all that the chief priests and elders had said to them. They then praised God for their release from jail, and the people raised their voices simultaneously, praying an astounding prayer that reached God. While they were engaging in prayer, a climactic event transpired: they were filled with the Holy Spirit, the meeting place was shaken, and they spoke with Holy boldness.

Corporate prayer causes the miraculous hand of God to pour out His Spirit on His sons and daughters, empowering them to witness tenaciously with uncompromising faith. This electrifying experience occurred because the saints were on one accord; praying and praising God, they petitioned Him to empower them with boldness to speak the unadulterated word of truth, and God granted their request.

The Upper Room Prayer

A harmonious prayer life exemplifies love, unity, and obedience to God. The upper room experience is a manifestation of the Divine impartation of the Holy Spirit that inspired and influenced the disciples to take a stance in their course of action. Jesus promised them a gift from His Father, and the Lord is faithful in delivering His promises. This corporate prayer meeting is an example of an intense, urgent cry to God for direction, strength, protection, and replacement of the disciple Judas. They (disciples) were all joined together constantly in prayer, with Jesus' mother, brothers, and godly women praying fervently in the upper room; they were obeying Jesus' instructions not to leave Jerusalem.

On the day of Pentecost, the Holy Spirit descended upon the disciple's, and they spoke in different languages. They had never before experienced this type of power. The endowment of the Holy Spirit empowered them to become international witnesses in Jerusalem, Judea, and Samaria, and to the ends of the world, compelling men, women, boys, and girls to accept Jesus as their risen Savoir. This was not a human power, but a supernatural power, which can only come from a sovereign God. The baptism of fire changed the course for evangelism, as the apostles' hearts were set aflame to perform the will of God. This scenario depicts the significance of the pinnacle of corporate prayer, which represents consecration of minds and hearts to bring unity in the Body of Christ.

Ezra the Scribe

Ezra, the priest, had a significant impact on the Jewish people. He studied the Torah, and he explicitly followed God's instructions, encouraging the Jews to pray for repentance and turn their hearts back to the Lord. Dismayed by their behavior, he confronted the Jewish people about interracial marriage with pagan women, and their disobedience for rebelling against God's law. He emphasized the significance of the law to the Jews so they could incorporate it into their lives to prevent their past mistakes from polluting their future.

Ezra led the Jews back to holiness, and they confessed their sins and engaged in corporate prayer and fasting to reaffirm their reliance and dependency on God. Prayer and fasting caused purification to occur, and prayer had a significant impact on their lives, convicting them of their sins, the promises of God, and His holiness. The Jewish people assembled in unity, strength, and like-mindedness to present a corporate prayer petition before the Lord, which illustrates true repentance.

In the presence of God is fullness of joy, and corporate prayers evolve with sincerity; they provide us with insight and solutions to specific problems. These problems can be resolved when saints wholeheartedly pray in concert. Prayerful Christians denounce, tear down, abolish, and destroy the demonic assignment of Satan, and God is pleased with the execution of their accomplishment.

God's majestic powers destroy works of iniquity. When we pray, "Our Father; which art in heaven," and say, "hallowed be thy name," we are reverencing the name of God. There is no other name superior to God! Our cries demand His personal attention. God opens up the windows in heaven and pours out bountiful blessings beyond our wildest imaginations. Demonic spirits are removed, ministries are developed, prosperity evolves, unity and love are exhibited in the congregation, souls are saved, and the kingdom of God is advanced. Corporate prayer represents unity in the house of God, obedience to the word of God, and commitment to prevail against Satan.

Corporate prayer assists saints to avoid the python spirit that restricts and prevents the Body of Christ from praying. Prayer strengthens us and edifies the house of God. It prevents divisiveness and releases spiritual gifts to be used in the Body of Christ, imparting a spirit of godliness that supersedes carnality. We must operate God's house as He ordained it to function and refrain from displaying defiant, rebellious, and disobedient behavior, which is non-productive and futile. The Bible proclaims, "For rebellion is as the sin of witchcraft, And stubbornness *is as* iniquity and idolatry" (1 Samuel 15:23 NKJV). Rebuke these spirits! The spirit of witchcraft and stubbornness must not enter into our churches. Refrain from polluting them with unruly conduct and wickedness. God detests this spirit of depravity, which breeds sin. Our objective is to pray and seek the face of God, asking for guidance to empower the church while continuing to exhibit love and demonstrate the bond of perfection.

Confrontations in the Church

Confrontations that occur in the church must be resolved quickly. Unresolved confrontations occur because of ungodliness and the differences in people's personalities and perspectives. These confrontations cause dissension in the church, leading disgruntled church members to change their memberships to different churches. Storefront churches are the result of controversies that were never resolved and eventually new churches began to emerge. In actuality, similar problems can resurface when they aren't addressed, leading discord to occur in the church.

Saints, don't waste your time fighting against one another; don't lose sight of our primary focus: salvation message. Pay attention to spiritual affairs; engage in prayer. We should be the activists who initiate petitions to put prayer back into the schools. We should be the flame of fire in our communities and schools, as well as our congregations, proclaiming that Jesus is Lord of our lives. Stand for righteousness, denouncing explicit sex on the television and the

Internet; prevent sexual perverts and predators from destroying our children's minds; and compel people to accept salvation. Young men and ladies have been deceived by the carnality of this world and have turned to alternative lifestyles: Johnny dating Jim, and Sally dating Sue. Satan is winning the war! The devil is a liar, though; God is still in control. Church leaders are falling by the wayside because of sin, and marriages are becoming a myth. Do not give Satan ammunition to destroy each other.

Be the ambassador who can teach the gospel, rebuke evil deeds, and confront evil works. Do not lose precious time and energy warring with each other in the church, permitting Satan the opportunity to cause controversy in the Body of Christ. Saints, strive to make a conscientious effort to resist opposition and embrace unity under the subjection of the Holy Spirit. Our battle has always been and always will be against Satan, so let's remain mindful of precisely who our opponents are. If we cannot get along on earth, how do we expect to rejoice in heaven? Acknowledge the good work of the early church. They sold their possessions and helped those who were in need; as a result, love for one another flourished in their hearts. The purpose of the church is to proclaim the gospel and compel men to come to Christ. Salvation is our message to a dying world, and let's not forget it.

Be cautious of these traps and remember that God is looking for churches without blemish or spot. He is looking for churches that have not lost their relationship with their first love and that will not compromise their faith while remaining prayerful through tribulation. He is actively searching for churches that are overcomers and that will prevail through adversities. God's spiritual spotlight is actively searching for churches that are alive and not dead, a reflection of Him and not the world. He is sending out an all-points bulletin for churches willing to endure tribulations, keep His Word, profess His name, and stand on His promises. He will reward the churches that are obedient, who rebuke and expose the antichrist, without compromising their faith. Is your church compliant with God's requirements?

God promises to give the churches that overcome a crown of life, hidden manna, white stone with a new name, pillar in the temple of God, authority over nations, and a morning star, as well as the right to sit with Him on the throne and be dressed in white (see Revelation chapters 2—3).

It has been unveiled to us in Revelation about the second coming of Jesus Christ. It behooves all Christians, backsliders, and sinners to heed the Word of God and act accordingly to His commandments so that He will not spew us out or say, "Depart from Me, all you workers of iniquity" (Luke 13:27 NKJV).

Be careful not to miss entering the kingdom of God because of your wicked, rebellious spirit or arrogant disposition. I do not want to be in a church that is blind, dumb, and nearsighted because God will remove it from His presence. Strive to be in God's kingdom and persevere to be with the saints, prophets, and the elders. God promised this inheritance to the believers, and we must not yield to temptation and always abide in the word of truth—no matter what the consequences entail. Adhere to God's plan, which He ordained, because judgment will literally begin at the church. Remember: our mission is salvation, propelled through prayer, and our enemy is Satan—not each other.

CHAPTER TWELVE

Spiritual Warfare

"He seized the dragon, that ancient serpent, who is the devil,
or Satan, and bound him for a thousand years."
Revelation 20:2

Accepting Jesus as our Lord and Savior automatically enlists us into His army; therefore, prepare to fight. God envisions His people joining an invincible army that never stands at ease; Christians must always stand at attention, forever alert and on guard for the demonic schemes, temptations, tactics, and lies deployed by Satan. Every Christian will encounter spiritual warfare—whether they are girded up with the whole armor of God or not. Trouble will come, and evil spirits will try to destroy, distort, and discourage you. Use the sword of the spirit, the gospel of Jesus Christ, and faithful prayers to rebuke and resist the devourer. God equips us with spiritual artillery to combat the enemy when we anticipate an attack.

Jail Ministry Warfare

Jail ministry is a challenging experience. Involvement takes dedication, persistence, patience, and prayer. You witness to rejected inmates who are menaces to society, yet a humbling interaction transpires when you're in their presence. They need God, and He is the only one capable of delivering them out of a dreary situation. Sister Lennie and I are dedicated in our involvement with the jail ministry. God has empowered us with the audacity to preach His word as we confront issues, impute wisdom where there is confusion, and teach the inmates about the gospel. Our intentions are to win souls for Christ and use spiritual weapons to cast out demonic spirits.

Each time we visit the inmates, Sister Lennie and I alternate on who will teach the lesson. On one particular visit, Sister Lennie was prepared to teach—when a satanic attack occurred unexpectedly during our jail ministry. Sister Lennie was wholeheartedly ministering to the women inmates about *how to pray*. As I glanced around the room, taking a surveillance of the women, I observed their facial expressions, body language, and whether or not they were involved in conversation. One particular woman drew my attention to her because of her disruptive spirit. While Lennie was lecturing, this particular inmate got out of her chair, walked casually to the front of the room where the literature was displayed on the table, took a Bible tract, then strutted back to her seat. As Lennie continued to lecture about prayer, I watched the disruptive inmate as she fidgeted in her seat and giggled during the lecture. Lennie continued to explain to the inmates the significance of incorporating prayer into their lives.

She said, "If you are unsure of how to pray, just say, '*The blood of Jesus*'—it will make demons tremble!"

The disruptive woman began to laugh hysterically during the lecture, vigorously raising her feet up and down off the floor and screaming, "The blood of Jesus, the blood of Jesus, ha, ha, ha, the blood of Jesus, the blood of Jesus, ha, ha, ha!" Suddenly, the women's attention shifted from listening to the lecture to focusing on the commotion that the inmate was making with her disruptive outburst and behavior. They were startled and couldn't decipher whether she was sincerely calling on the name of Jesus or mocking what Lennie had instructed them to do. The Holy Spirit revealed to me that she possessed a demonic spirit, the same spirit displayed by a fortune-telling slave girl who followed Paul and Silas and his followers while they were going to the place of prayer. The slave girl shouted, "These men are servants of the Most High God, who are telling you the way to be saved." She kept this commotion up for many days until Paul finally became troubled in his spirit. He then spoke to the spirit within her and said, "In the name of Jesus Christ, I command you to come out of her!" At that moment, the spirit left her (Acts 16:16-18).

The demonic spirit in the room troubled me as I observed the erratic behavior of the inmate. The smirk on her face, her high-pitched voice, and her repetitious actions of racing up her feet demonstrated to me that she was mocking God! This was the same spirit illustrated in the Bible in Acts. I put some anointing oil on my hands, and before I knew it, I walked swiftly over to her seat while she continued to disrupt the class. I placed my hand on her forehead and said, "In the name of Jesus, Satan, I rebuke you!" The attention of the class shifted from the inmate to me, and everyone was startled—including the lecturer. As soon as I spoke, the inmate reacted just as I thought she would: she got up out of her seat and said loudly, "Why are you singling me out!" Her behavior changed from elation to anger, and I knew it was a satanic attack because the Holy Spirit revealed it to me. I immediately told everyone to get up out of their seats and start praying. They all complied—except the disruptive inmate—joining hands in a circle as instructed, including Lennie, who was standing in front of the classroom, baffled. I instructed one of the inmates to lead us in prayer, and she complied, falling on her knees and sincerely saying, *"Father, I don't know what to pray for,"* as tears streamed down her face. As she began to pray, I knew God was present because of Romans 8:26 (NKJV), my favorite Scripture: "Likewise the Spirit also helps in our weaknesses. For we do not know what we should pray for as we ought, but the Spirit Himself makes intercession for us with groanings which cannot be uttered." For me, that was confirmation from God acknowledging that He had the situation under control.

The Spirit of God rose up in me to rebuke the devourer's evil spirit, and we were suddenly engaged in spiritual warfare because of Lennie's discourse about the blood of Jesus—but I was determined not to lose. "When anyone hears the message about the kingdom and does not understand it, the evil one comes and snatches away what was sown in his heart. This is the seed sown along the path" (Matthew 13:19). Seeds sown in prayer and the blood of Jesus are spiritual nourishment for the soul. Spiritual discernment empowered me to operate under the anointing, preventing Satan from stealing God's precious Word. The heart is the central core of man's desire; man's heart is the fertile ground in which the Word of God takes root. Satan's objective is to intercept God's Word. Satan's intentions are to prevent these women from obtaining salvation by infusing confusion into their minds and preventing them from hearing the gospel. Satan understands that the blood of Jesus is a powerful and effective weapon against his kingdom, and so do I.

Finally, the disruptive inmate began to calm down; I remained attentive to everyone's movement in the room and observed the expressions on the faces of the women who were praying. Suddenly, the Holy Spirit took control, and a profound spirit of worship emerged. After the prayer, the entire room was tranquil, and you could hear a pin drop. I then began to shout, "Hallelujah!" as Lennie began to speak in tongues. The women returned to their seats, wiping the tears from their eyes. Meanwhile, the disruptive inmate sat quietly and composed in her seat. After the *Shekinah* glory of God departed the room, the women were in awe of what they had witnessed. One of them finally said softly, "Truly, the LORD has been in this place." Lennie then finished her lecture and dismissed the class.

Spiritual warfare comes when you least expect it, whether at the hour of prayer or while teaching about the *Blood of Jesus*. God gives us discernment about the enemy's divisive tactics so we can take authority over them. God has empowered us to stand victoriously against the devil and to step harshly on and over Satan, denying the evil spirit to rise again—leaving it powerless.

Who is the enemy?

Our battle is against the greatest deceiver of humanity. Spiritual warfare is against Satan, Lucifer, devil, Beelzebub, ferocious lion, cunning serpent, dragon, prince of the air, demonic spirit, adversary, son of perdition, imitator of lights, and the spirit of darkness that projects evil spirits. Let's not make any mistakes about what his name is; he is the greatest imitator, deceiver, liar, thief, con artist, and counterfeiter that ever prowled the earth.

In Genesis, he is revealed as a cunning serpent that deceived Eve in the botanical garden. He tempted Jesus in the wilderness and enticed Judas to befriend Jesus in the garden of Gethsemane with the kiss of death. His deceptive and dangerous encounter with Eve led to the downfall of humanity, which allowed sin to enter into the world due to disobedience. Satan's capability to exploit humanity and confuse spiritual instructions reveals that he is clever, crafty, and deadly.

Revelation 9:11 asserts that he is known as Abaddon, Apollyon, the angel of the bottomless pit that possesses demonic power. He trespassed in heaven, and God cast him down to earth. He continuously makes accusation against the saints, attempting to jeopardize our salvation. He accused Job of being righteous to God because of his possessions and wealth. In Zechariah 3:1, he made an accusation about Joshua, who was a symbolic representation of the nation of Israel, for committing sin and being filthy in the presence of the Lord. This vindictive plaintiff introduces trumped-up evidence about our conduct, character, and behavior before a holy and righteous God, so do not provide him with any forensic evidence to present to God that will defame your character.

Peter warns the brethren to "Be self-controlled and alert. Your enemy—the devil—prowls around like a roaring lion looking for someone to devour" (1 Peter 5:8). This Scripture identifies three characteristics of Satan: he is the adversary, devil, and roaring lion. Adversary is our opponent; "devil" means "slander, an individual who desires to succeed in scandalizing your character"; and roaring lion is symbolic representation of Satan's ability to kill anyone who wars against him.

Satan is a roaring lion who will destroy your life. He is the opponent that will attack us physically, spiritually, and mentally in order to tear us apart. Satan opposes the work of God, and Christians must be alert and sober in order to discern his deceptive and cruel tactics. He lurks around earth to discern the evil deeds in which people are involved, and he entices and tempts individuals in order to devastate their lives.

Satan is the prince of demons, he has authority over demonic spirits in the heaven and earth realm, and he does not operate alone. A ruler over demonic spirits is vicious and destructive, and his mission is to destroy God's people and His kingdom. Jesus foreknew this and spiritually cleansed the temple when He cast out demons capable of destroying people's lives.

Another name for Satan is Belial, which means "vile and wicked, one who is capable of causing destruction." When Paul witnessed to the Corinthians, he made an inquiry about Christ: "And what accord has Christ with Belial? Or what does a believer with an unbeliever?" Satan is also known as Belial, who has the power to destroy your life when you defiantly walk in disobedience. Christ is antagonistic to every scheme Belial designs. Every Christian must proceed with caution in order to avoid contact with Belial. Our Savior does not keep company with the enemy, and neither should we.

John proclaims that anyone who does not believe that Jesus manifests himself in the flesh is as an antichrist. Imminent danger awaits us when we follow Satan's deceptive advice; this spirit is not of Christ, but it is characteristic of the antichrist. His intention is to confuse, belittle, and antagonize God's people, and his objective is to prevail against the power of God. Our attentiveness helps us to detect Satan's brutal attacks; we must watch and pray to avert temptation and destruction from the enemy.

Matthew 6:13 emphasizes, "Lead us not unto temptation but deliver us from the evil one." This passage depicts a plea for deliverance and protection from Satan. God does not tempt us—Satan does. Evil works are the manifestation of Satan, who is the culprit devising the scheme. The only one capable of leading and guiding us from evil is God; He makes the steps of the righteous man firm. Pray and divert from walking into temptation that steers you away from God. Temptation causes us to walk in darkness instead of God's light, and darkness is capable of causing detriment to our well-being.

Satan camouflages himself in different disguises to entice you. He is the god of this age who has blinded the eyes of people to believe that there is no God. These people are perishing, and they lack wisdom and truth. The fool says in his heart, "There is no God." They are corrupt, and their ways are vile; there is no one who does good (Psalm 53:1). Foolish people believe that this statement is true, because Satan has bamboozled them. But wise men seek God, and the heavens declare His glory. Spiritual blindness prevents people from obtaining faith and the revelation of the deity of God. Satan has followers whose minds are set on committing wicked acts and enticing others to practice their demonic ways. They are full of envy, murder, strife, deceit, and malice. They are gossips, slanderers, God-haters, insolent, arrogant, and boastful; they invent ways of doing evil; they disobey their parents; they are senseless, faithless, heartless, and ruthless. Satan is the father to those who choose to perform these hideous acts (Romans 1:29—30). These people commit acts that are an abomination unto Jehovah, and their intentions are to harm you.

Every day, we witness malicious crimes committed in our society. Drive-by shootings, rapes, molestation, domestic violence, and ballistic shootings on college campuses, in the workplace, and in shopping malls. Our churches have also felt the sting of death when worshipers have experienced shooting sprees in their congregations. Mourners are horrified when gang members shoot into a memorial service and they witness another fatal shooting. Satan is the mastermind behind these horrific crimes.

Satan is a murderer and a liar; there is no truth in him. When he speaks a lie, he speaks from his own resources. His followers are a replica of him. They represent deceit, darkness, and demonic intentions. Jesus identifies the Jewish leaders as demonic when they follow the ways of the devil. Their deeds were orchestrated in darkness, and their intention was to kill Jesus—the light. Instead of the Jewish leaders guiding the Jews to Christ, they led them straight to Satan, wandering into spiritual depravity.

Satan is the prince of the power of the air, and people who walk according to his demands are sons of perdition. These wicked, spineless individuals are thoughtless, cold-blooded murders who relish in performing evil deeds. They gloat in their disobedience because of the spiritual darkness that dwells within them. They do not fear, obey, or reverence God. Satan's work is visibly seen in their corrupt lives. He destroys their souls and controls their minds by his devious power; they are consciously enthralled with performing evil deeds.

Satan is a sifter who desires to determine our faith in God. He asked for God's permission to sift Peter as wheat. Sifting is an act of examining and sorting carefully. I imagine Satan wanted to decipher Peter's true character to determine whether he was a man of God or an imposter led by fleshly desires and an impulsive agenda. Jesus graciously interceded in prayer for Peter, He prayed for Peter's faith to prevail and sustain him; he did not want Peter to waver in his faith because faltering leads to uncertainty about one's belief. Jesus' prayer kept the enemy from devouring Peter. When Jesus intercedes in prayer for the believer, He accomplishes "His will." He perceived Peter's potential to become the apostolic leader of the Jewish community, counterattacking Satan's demonic intentions. Satan is incapable of succeeding in his destructive schemes against God's people.

Satan, the dragon, caused chaos in heaven, and a spiritual warfare occurred among him and his angels against the heavenly host. Satan fought vehemently against God and His angels, eventually cast down from a prominent position in heaven. Satan is also known as Lucifer, a Hebrew name that literally means "Day Star." God is the only bright and morning star that has dominion in heaven and earth, and no imposter can take His place. Satan's desire was to exalt his throne above the stars of the Most High. Satan is known as the angel of lights. His lights are composed of glitz and glamour that detour people to travel down a road that leads to destruction and ultimately destroys their lives. Jesus is the light of the world—A light that never loses its brilliance! Satan masquerades himself as an angel of light, and his servants masquerade as servants of righteousness. Satan is the imitator of false lights, incapable of comparison with Jesus. Do not be persuaded by his tactics. Rebuke Satan adamantly each time you encounter his conniving schemes in your homes, churches, jobs, or relationships, and thoughts. James 4:7 says, "Resist the devil and he will flee from you." Are you resisting Satan or being led by him?

Our Defense

Who is this King of glory? The LORD strong and mighty, the LORD mighty in battle (Psalm 24:8). The LORD is our defense against all satanic attacks and encounters, and as Christian soldiers, we must abide by the rules and regulations of Christ to be victorious. Christians' participation in spiritual warfare is not an option. When you are enlisted in the army of God, it is your spiritual obligation to finish your course. God has devised a strategic defense that is spiritually aggressive against Satan; you're authorized to use the power that God has endowed in you against him.

How can we overcome Lucifer? How can we destroy strongholds? Revelation 12:11 says, "And they overcome Satan by the blood of the Lamb and by the word of their testimony." Our spiritual weapons against the enemy are the blood of Jesus, our testimonies, our prayers, praise and worship, and God's Word. The blood covers all sins—past, present, and future—and understanding this biblical principle gives us remarkable insight to fight with valor and dignity. Do not be intimidated or disillusioned: God is triumphant against Satan, and He needs warriors who are not afraid to fight. God empowers us to confront Satan before he attacks us, and spiritual discernment combined with prayer gets the job done—regardless of the difficulty of the assignment.

CHAPTER THIRTEEN

Armor of God

"Put on the full armor of God so that you can take your stand
against the devil's schemes."
Ephesians 6:11

Jesus has revealed our enemy, and we must be mindful to discern when demonic forces are at work. Resist the devil! Proclaim the Word of God, and the blood of Jesus will assist in making him flee. Jesus triumphantly defeated and crushed the serpent head at the cross; therefore, we have victory in Christ Jesus. Hallelujah! We must stand firm and fight a courageous battle. God has designed a Divine armor to defeat Satan and his angels, and we must use it.

Ephesians 6:10–18 states, "Finally, be strong in the Lord and in his mighty power. Put on the full armor of God so that you can take your stand against the devil's schemes. For our struggle is not against flesh and blood, but against the rulers, against the authorities, against the powers of this dark world and against the spiritual forces of evil in the heavenly realms. Therefore put on the full armor of God, so that when the day of evil comes, you may be able to stand your ground, and after you have done everything, to stand. Stand firm then, with the belt of truth buckled around your waist, with the breastplate of righteousness in place, and with your feet fitted with the readiness that comes from the gospel of peace. In addition to all of this, take up the shield of faith, with which you can extinguish all the flaming arrows of the evil one. Take the helmet of salvation and the sword of the Spirit, which is the word of God. And pray in the Spirit on all occasions with all kinds of prayers and requests. With this in mind, be alert and always keep on praying for all the saints."

This invaluable armor is precious, and everyone cannot wear God's apparel; the armor is specifically designed for believers. Ephesians 6:10 gives us explicit instructions to be strong in the Lord and His power, not ours. God possesses omnipotent power in heaven, earth, and the sea below. He has dominion over everything. Paul discerned the importance of being strong in the Lord and His omnipotent power. Paul fought and stood firm against Lucifer's schemes and used the gospel efficaciously. While visiting Lystra, Paul encountered vengeful men who came from Antioch and Iconium. These perverted men persuaded the crowd to stone Paul, and they dragged him outside the city, where they presumed he was dead.

Can you picture Jesus telling Paul to "Get up, get up! They don't understand what caliber of man you are! They meant to harm you, but I am turning this situation around for your good! Go back and tear down, annihilate every stronghold and demonic power that exists. I am the Lord, strong and mighty, victorious in all battles"? The disciples stood around Paul as he lay on the ground. The resurrected power of God then raised Paul up. He returned to the city reenergized to preach the gospel with authority and power, unintimidated by the men and the evil spirits that caused him detriment. The Scripture proclaims, "For it is God who works in you to will and act according to His good purpose" (Philippians 2:13). God will resurrect you from a dead situation with power, rejuvenation, and vigor to walk in victory against Satan's evil scheme. God is inquisitive about how much faith and stamina we possess. Faithful Paul understood that Satan's intentions were to kill him, but his assignment was to proclaim the gospel of Jesus Christ. Although Paul was unconscious, God revived him to a conscious state. He possessed the will to overpower Satan by returning to the city. Paul had not lost the battle because he had been knocked down. He got up with the intention to defeat Satan with the sword of the spirit. Paul realized that Lucifer had won Round 1, but greater is He that is in me than in the world. Paul deciphered that the battle was not over until God said it was over. God is able to shed light to expose vindictive plots. Therefore, we must possess the same tenacity to prevail against Lucifer, using the "rope-a-dope" technique that sharpens our mentality while letting us take a breather against the ropes. This strategic plan allows us time to recuperate and come back with a spiritual flurry of explosive blows. When Jesus raised Paul up to a conscious state, Round 2 began and Paul visualized himself as the winner and Satan as a defeated foe.

We don't scrimmage with our enemy; we win the battle. Our fight is primarily against spiritual rulers of darkness, wickedness, and authorities who possess evil powers against the heavenly realm. We do not war against flesh and blood and Paul knew this. Those who are made of flesh and blood are humans, and those who are not are demons. There is a vast distinction between the two. Be cautious about whom this spiritual warfare is against because our opponent is Satan, who is always behind the scene aggravating the situation.

We consistently wrestle against principalities, powers, rulers of darkness, and spiritual wickedness in the heavenly realms. Principalities are orders of angels, supramundane powers in conflict with God. They consist of a hierarchy of spiritual ranks and authority that descends from heaven to the earth realm. Satanic powers tempt people to engage in ruthless acts that are cruel and detrimental to others. They participate in the occult, palm reading, Ouija board, tarot cards, fortune telling, divination, reading horoscopes, blood sacrifices, witchcraft, lasciviousness, idolatry, gothic involvement, and terrorism. Satan is evil and wicked, and as the ruler of darkness, he denounces and antagonizes Christians. Wickedness implies an appetite to commit evil deeds in which people indulge for pleasure.

Our fight is spiritual and descends from the heavenly realm; we wrestle with an invisible opponent who is capable of causing detriment. "Wrestle" means to struggle for mastery and power. We are entangled by and in close proximity with the enemy. Our aim is to throw our opponents off balance and destroy them by moving or lifting our adversaries from their respective positions. We immobilize their positions by pinning them down with the Word of God and leaving them defenseless by the power of the Holy Spirit. Saints take advantage of their adversaries by tearing down strongholds, shedding light on darkness, and removing spiritual wickedness. This is accomplished by sharing the gospel, our testimonies, prayer and fasting, corporate and individual prayer, intercessory prayer, God's Word, rebuking Satan, and praying at the location where the crime or sin occurred. Our objective is to paralyze, incapacitate, or destroy our enemies by any means necessary.

Satan is notorious, but God is victorious against iniquitous conduct. Consistently defeating Satan entails following God's commandments, doctrinal truth, and using weapons of mass destruction (our Bible's) that cause significant fatality to demonic terrain. Our weapons are not carnal but mighty to the pulling down of strongholds, and everything that is not like God is destroyed. We vehemently charge the enemy with swirling swords and shout, "We come in the name of the Lord God Almighty," imitating King David when he confronted Goliath and victoriously killed the enemy with his slingshot.

When we become serious about our Father's business, He will become serious about our problems. Someone's life may depend upon your dedication and vigilance to withstand the enemy. Deploy a spirit of victory against the enemy for the sake of humanity. God's armor is effective and powerful against Satan. The armor is a reflection of God's spiritual power, and it's used both offensively and defensively to combat demonic forces. Wearing the armor protects us from our opponents' attacks, and it facilitates us in standing firm against the opposition during spiritual warfare. God's armor is described below.

Belt of Truth

The belt of truth stabilizes our position in Christ, denounces the wicked spirit of Satan, and makes provision for the saints to shame the devil by revealing the truth that exposes his lies. Lying is an abomination to God. He is the way, truth, and life. He is the way to enter into heaven, the truth that will set us free, and He is eternal life, which we receive because of our faith in Him. God hates a liar. We must gravitate away from lies and exhibit truth. No liar will enter into heaven, and since Satan is the father of lies, it is our responsibility to denounce his fabrications.

Breastplate of Righteousness

The breastplate of righteousness protects our vital organs, and any arrow that hits the breastplate is deflected. The breastplate of righteousness is a replica of God's character. He is righteous and just, and His expectation is for the saints to reflect Him. Because of the blood of Jesus, God's unmerited favor pardons our sins and places us in right standing with Him. God imputed righteousness in us; therefore, we must live according to His Word and be upright before His presence, being mindful that our standard of conduct is righteousness. Blessings crown the head of the righteous because they seek to do good.

Gospel Shoes

During any war, soldiers must wear the appropriate shoes for combat in order to aid movement and reposition themselves against the enemy; likewise, we must never falter, keeping ourselves steadfast and unmovable targets. When we shod our feet with the gospel, we are obligated to tell the "good news" about our Lord and Savior Jesus Christ. Romans 10:15 (NKJV) As it is written, "How beautiful are the feet of those who preach the gospel of peace, Who bring glad tidings of good things!" Jesus' desire is for us to evangelize the nations, preaching the gospel to all people who will compel their hearts to accept Jesus as their personal Savior. Christianity gives us an assurance of hope that only exists in the salvation of Jesus Christ, and shodding our feet with the gospel while heralding Jesus' salvation plan pleases the Lord.

Shield of Faith

The shield of faith is Jesus Christ's protection against the spirit of wickedness. This powerful shield protects our armor and deflects any arrows meant to injure us. The shield of faith has the spiritual fire retardant necessary to extinguish all fiery darts deployed by the enemy. This shield equips us to fight spiritually against a demonic force that reigns in darkness and delights in pervasiveness. It also has the authoritative power to fend off the enemy while conquering its territory. Because of the shield of faith, we are able to withstand the fire, no matter how hot the intensity of the flames may become. "Faith" can conquer anything.

Helmet of Salvation

Salvation is found in no one else, for there is no other name under heaven given to men by which we must be saved (Acts 4:12). Salvation is a personal acceptance of Jesus Christ, who reconciled us back with God. Because of salvation, we wear helmets to protect our intellects, or psyches. The helmet of salvation protects the head from the vicious blows of Satan. Blunt trauma to the cranium can cause injury to the brain stem and leave a person in a vegetative state. Isaiah emphasizes, "You will keep in perfect peace him whose mind is steadfast, because he trusts in you" (Isaiah 26:3).

Our minds are perfect embodiments of the mind of Christ. The sound mind is free from confusion or becoming double-minded; it is a fearless mind capable of rebuking Satan on his own turf. Our minds concentrate on walking in faith, believing the outcome will be victorious. A powerful mind that sees beyond the natural into the spiritual realm is capable of making demons tremble. This blessed mind gives God the praise for the strength He has empowered in us to tread, walk, and stomp on Lucifer.

Sword of the Spirit

The sword of the spirit is the Word of God! He is the living Word! For the Word of God is living and active. Sharper than any double-edged sword, it penetrates even to dividing soul and spirit, joints and marrow; it judges the thoughts and attitudes of the heart (Hebrews 4:12). The sword of the spirit possesses the ability to cut down and through anything that defies God's Word. We do not have to fear the evil acts that men commit because they will perish by the sword. God has made a provision for us to use His sword to cut down spiritual wickedness, principalities, and rulers of darkness. God's Word accomplishes its mission; His Word specifically achieves prophetic results because it was sent with power and authority.

Matthew 4:4 proclaims, "Jesus answered and said, "It is written: 'Man does not live on bread alone, but by every word that comes from the mouth of God.'" Jesus used the Word of God against Satan to illustrate to the believers just how effective His Word is. God's Word is a powerful weapon that exudes a force with which Satan is incapable of stopping. God's Word accomplishes what it is sent out to perform, and no one can destroy the Word of God. In the beginning was the Word, and the Word was with God, and the Word was God (John 1:1).

Using the Word of God against Satan ignites a power that Satan cannot defeat. The psalmist advises us to hide the Word in our hearts, and then we will be equipped to deploy it against Satan efficiently. God's Word cast out demonic spirits, dried up issues of bleeding, healed leprosy, and imparted sight to blind men. The sword is the only offensive weapon that we can execute with force. It is serious, deadly, and necessary to use against Satan to destroy spiritual wickedness. Use the sword effectively.

Intensity of Warfare

Warfare is serious and deadly; therefore, be alert! It is not a myth, but a reality. Satan lures people into places he wants you to go, where he has booby traps lying in wait for you to set off. Beware: Satan disguises and camouflages himself to blend in with society, but the spirit of discernment exposes his vile schemes, enabling you to execute every demonic spirit that is antagonistic to God. Don't be afraid or intimidated; stand your ground. Defend yourself! Maintain a warrior's mentality; realize you are spiritually equipped to defeat Satan and that you are in this battle to win it. God sends people into Satan's camp to infiltrate his domain to rescue people who are literally trapped in the war zone—your assignment is to save them. God needs spiritual sharp shooters and task force servants who are capable of warring relentlessly against Satan, Lucifer, the dragon, serpent, etc.

Take warfare seriously, realizing tangible weapons are ineffective against spiritual darkness. God's armor is used to fight against an invisible army whose objective is to kill, steal, and destroy every child of God. Be vigilant and submissive to God's instructions, realizing there will be casualties when you engage in battle. But if you follow God's commands explicitly, you won't be the victim. Note: spiritual warfare is not against humans, but against spiritual wickedness, and rulers of darkness. Fight the good fight and keep the faith, finishing your course like Paul. Wear the entire armor with dignity, self-control, and pride. You never know when Lucifer will attack you; never remove your armor. Fight courageously and be faithfully committed to God, and pray with an intensity of fire.

CHAPTER FOURTEEN

Pray and Do Not Faint

"Then He spoke a parable to them,
that men always ought to pray and not lose heart."
Luke 18:1 (NKJV)

Throughout history, devout Jewish men have prayed in accordance with the will of God and kept His ordinance. Their prayers caused God to glance at the bloody doorpost and pass over the Israelites' homes, produce manna to fall from heaven, water to spring forth from a rock, quail to fall from the sky, the sun to stand still, a raging sea to become tranquil, dry bones to be resuscitated, and armies to retreat from battle. Their prayers regulated the temperature in a fiery furnace, cast out demons, restored spiritual life to a dying nation, and caused blessings to reign upon ungodly people.

God desires righteous men who can pray and authorizes them to enter into the inner court to prevail in ardent prayer, without malice or contempt in their hearts. They offer the sacrifice of praise with the fruit of their lips. Their prayers hinge on God's promises, and they have witnessed the movement of God in their lives. Their sentiment is the driving force that propels their prayers, and their sanctified lives illustrate their harmony with God.

Devout men who pray display sacred lives that honor God. They discern when to pray, how to pray, and to whom to pray. Not every man can be entrusted to pray, but righteous men adhere to the Word of God, explicitly vowing not to falter; they realize the detriment that can occur because of prayerlessness. They consecrate themselves spiritually unto the Lord while meditating on His Word as their souls thirst to hear God speak. The anointing moves them into a spiritual dimension that leads them to extol God. The prayers of men that have clean hands and purity within their hearts delight God as He confirms that He has heard their supplications. Godly men display purpose driven lives that encompass prayer. This reality vividly reveals their zeal to acquaint themselves with God as vessels of power. Men should always pray, without excuses, because God can use them as vehicles to touch people's lives.

Where prayerlessness resides, disaster awaits. Men who are reluctant to pray effectively have lives that lead to avenues of uncertainties that eventually cause them to sin or become fainthearted. Throughout the Bible, people of God fainted due to unbearable circumstances beyond their control. The Hebrew word for "faint" is *Ya'aph* (yaw-ef'), which means "to become fatigued, exhausted, or weary."[12] When men faint, they cease to pray; when men pray, they cease to faint. There is a grave difference between the two. Prayer strengthens us, but faintness weakens our position. To faint means that one is under pressure, enormous stress, and opposition. We become apprehensive and discontented. To faint means literally to lose spiritual strength, insight, and power. Faintness reveals our human vulnerabilities, which exhibit despondence, lethargy, incoherence, and dismay. God never told us that we would not faint. He instructed us to pray and faint not. Remember God's Word. Psalm 27:1 declares, "The LORD is my light and my salvation—whom shall

I fear? The LORD is the stronghold of my life—of whom shall I be afraid?" Fear not—God is with you! Your anxieties and fears are nailed to the cross. Do not be anxious about situations you cannot change or control, but rather engage in prayer consistently. Prayer is the shield and buckler that prevents bouts of faintness from entering into our lives. Unlike prayer, faintness leaves us hopeless and unable to ascertain alternatives to our situations. Our flesh fears the unknown, and a spirit of doom and gloom overshadows us.

The Shunammite woman was in bitter distress due to her son's death. She sought the man of God, Elisha, for an answer. "I would have lost heart, unless I had believed—That I would see the goodness of the LORD— In the land of the living" (Psalm 27:13 NKJV). She witnessed the anointing power of God manifested through Elisha as he resurrected her son from the dead, and this miraculous miracle prevented her from becoming fainthearted.

Hannah was downhearted and wept bitterly because she was barren and fainthearted. She would not eat and was grief-stricken about her sterility. In her anguish, she poured out her soul to the Lord and discovered serenity through prayer. The Lord blessed her womb, and she conceived a male child. She named him Samuel and dedicated him to the Lord. Her spirit of discontentment then dissipated. God listened to her prayer and alleviated her despair.

The Bible depicts a vivid illustration of the vulnerability of Jesus' temptation in the desert by Satan. This wilderness experience exhibits Jesus as being fully man and fully God. He experienced physical fatigue, hunger, and loneliness during his forty days and forty nights of fasting, so God dispensed His angels to minister to Jesus' famished body and weakened spirit. The Word of God sustained Him to rebuke the devourer, and He adamantly refused to bow to Satan.

Peter exhorted, "Beloved, do not think it strange concerning the fiery trial which is to try you, as though some strange thing happened to you" (1 Peter 4:12 NKJV). It is not strange that the opposition will come against you. Satan tempted Jesus—the son of God! He will tempt you. You are Satan's prime target, and he wants to destroy you. These fiery trials are not strange; they are confirmation of the Word of God. He informed us that we would have tribulations, which implies that we will experience extreme trials and opposition in our lives. We lift up our eyes to the hill – where does our help come from? My help comes from the LORD, the Maker of heaven and earth (Psalm 121:1—2). He is our help in the time of trouble. We trust Him because He is faithful and true. We must trust God in difficult situations, trust God when it looks hopeless, trust God when we are in despair, and trust Him when we are faint and weary. He alone possesses supernatural power that will lift broken spirits and mend broken hearts.

Ecclesiastes 3:1 explains, "There is a time for everything, and a season for every activity under heaven." Life can be wonderful one moment, and the next moment, it suddenly spirals downward, dramatically changing your life, and leaving you perplexed about the situation. Fainting is an unforeseen event that can occur in anyone's life. With each occurrence of fainting, prayer is the antidote prescribed to alleviate the symptoms.

I experienced faintheartedness one Sunday morning at church. The pastor called for altar prayer. As I walked out of the choir stand, tears were streaming down my face. I continued to walk quietly to the altar for prayer; several of my sisters in Christ noticed me crying and embraced me at the altar. One of the sisters said, "Cover her" they discerned that I was troubled. Two of my sisters in Christ stood beside me, and one stood in front of me. As I leaned on the shoulder of the sister standing next to me, I held my head down. When altar prayer was finished, I did not return to the choir stand; instead, I sat in the pew, accompanied by these women.

I distinctly remember crying softly throughout the service, which was unusual for me. I continued to hold my head down as the tears flowed nonstop down my face. Although I did not cry out audibly, it was evident that I was distressed. As I was crying, the tears dropped onto the page that was opened in my Bible. Looking through my cloudy vision, I read the Scripture, "And let us not grow weary while doing good, for in due season we shall reap if we do not lose heart" (Galatians 6:9 NKJV). God spoke to me in that Scripture; He was revealing to me that I was fainting; He perceived I was disappointed and that Satan had attacked me from every angle with his fiery darts. He also understood I would recover but that I needed time to recollect my thoughts, gather my strength, and understand why I was in spiritual warfare.

God's intention was not for me to have a pity party. I knew that there were two options to my trials: either I was going to succumb to the problem, or the trial would strengthen me and make me strong. Proverbs 24:10 exclaims that if you falter in times of trouble, how small is your strength. My strength was dwindling fast. I had to resist the enemy with every ounce of my being; so having recognized the problem, I went to the problem solver (Jesus). I realized I had to rise above the situation to overcome this calamitous event.

I've read that verse before, but this time it resonated in my spirit. God was testing my ability to stand against the wiles of the devil, and I needed to stand courageously against him even though I was disheartened. How do I escape from a troubled heart when I see the carnality in children who are reared in Christian homes? How can I prevent my heart from aching when I tried my best to be obedient to God and stand for righteousness? How do I recuperate from awesome blows that crushed my spirit? How can I stand against the enemy with depleted energy? What will prevent me from spiritually collapsing?

The Holy Spirit reminded me that He gives strength to the weary and increases the power of the weak (Isaiah 40:29). God replenishes depleted energy. Instantaneous strength comes from the Lord! Therefore, I began to encourage myself while meditating on the Word of God. I began to call things that were not as though they were (Romans 4:17). I began to speak life into my children's lives. Faith equips me to endure trials and inspires me to overcome bouts of faintness with confidence. "No weapon forged against you will prevail, and you will refute every tongue that accuses you. This is the heritage of the servants of the LORD, and this is their vindication from me, declares the LORD" (Isaiah 54:17). I am an heir to the King; therefore, I will not live beneath my privileges. I believe the Word of God is true. Weapons of lies, mistrust, confusion, and disappointment will form, but they will not accomplish their cynical mission of destruction.

No matter what the journey may entail, I must diligently persevere. I continually walk by faith, refusing to focus on the things that I visualize. I realized that God's presence is apparent in my darkest encounter. He is present when I am in despair, present when it appears like a no-win situation. He is present when I am elated and when I am sad. God is an omnipresent God that has promised to be with me even until the end of the world. I had to seek refuge in God to strengthen myself for the battles that lay ahead. I needed God to restore my soul, and restoration began when I separated myself from my family and sought God as a refuge in prayer.

Jesus proclaimed, "These things I have spoken to you, that in Me you may have peace. In the world you will have tribulation; but be of good cheer, I have overcome the world" (John 16:33 NKJV). The Greek word for "tribulation" is *thlipsis* which means "pressure, affliction, distress, or trouble."[13] Jesus has overcome the trouble of this world. He knew He would encounter trouble, pressure, and distress, but it did not hinder His Divine assignment to search for lost souls. His ministry had just begun, and quitting was not an option. Jesus implemented prayer early in His ministry, which kept Him connected to God. He prayed in the desert, at the transfiguration, for the future Christian, and on the cross at Calvary. Jesus left vivid schemata, displaying how He prayed in the garden of Gethsemane. He prayed until His sweat was like blood. He prayed an agonizing prayer—not once, but three times. He sought reassurance from God by saying, "Not my will, but let thy will be done." Despite His anguish, He fulfilled the assignment, believing that prayer reveals the attitude of His heart and intentions of His soul. Despite the obstacles that existed in His life, Jesus displayed dedication and commitment.

We must establish a prayer life similar to Christ's. Persistence in prayer supplies us with sustaining power, reminding us never to quit the assignment prior to its completion. We must ask ourselves these questions: Are we willing to pray until we are confident we are operating in the will of God? Are we willing to pray during uncomfortable circumstances? Are we willing to pray alone, even though tired and sleepy believers accompany us? Are we willing to pray when we are weary and faint? Someone has to be committed to pray in situations that are stressful, uncomfortable, and cause us to sweat. We must learn God's will and pray for its profound manifestation to operate in our lives, churches, schools, communities, and government.

Prayer should be in the forefronts of our minds as we plead with God for a response. If God does not answer the first time, pray again. If God does not answer the second time, pray again. If God does not answer the third time, maintain a prayerful spirit. The Holy Spirit will hold our prayers up as a banner before the presence of God, interceding with moans, groans, and utterances. The Holy Spirit ensures that our prayers are congruent with the Word of God. Like Jesus, I wholeheartedly believe that God will answer our prayers and perfect the things concerning our welfare.

What does a person do when they are oblivious to the fact that they are in a fainting state? No one is exempt from bouts of fainting; it occurs suddenly and without warning. Each situation is different, but the similarity and symptoms for fainting remain congruent:

mentally, you are concentrating on the problem; physically, you are in a weakened state, which causes you to agonize over the problem; spiritually, you are in despair, and your vulnerability causes you to lose focus on the spiritual manifestation of God. Outside pressures often causes internal pain. God is observant, and He recognizes our dilemma. He is the only wise God able to keep us from collapsing, the only one capable of perfecting our weaknesses beyond our comprehension. The sufficiency of His grace transforms our lives, perfects our weaknesses, and imparts strength. God will not tremensdous burdens on us that we are incapable of bearing. Unbearable situations test our strength. We don't realize how strong we are until we experience pressure or problems that we cannot solve or change. God tests our characters to determine our responses and ascertain if we can withstand the taxing situations.

When we experience bouts of weariness and fainting, Jesus stands with His arms wide open, beckoning us to come to Him, illustrating His expression of love. "Come to me, all you who are weary and burdened, and I will give you rest" (Matthew 11:28). Resting in the Lord means complete tranquility from the bombardment of the problems of this world. He gives us rest that rejuvenates us spiritually to combat stressful situations. When we encounter faintness, restoration comes from God.

When we begin to faint, we must remember the cross. Look at the cross; take a panoramic observation of Jesus' commitment and obedience to His Father for humanity and the sacrifices that Jesus made for us. Jesus never ceased praying, even when he endured agony, pain, and ridicule. He never stops thinking about his loved ones. He left us a vivid illustration of obedience, dedication, love, prayer, and salvation by praying, "Father, forgive them, for they do not know what they are doing" (Luke 23:34). His atoning blood gives us the tenacity to overcome detriment, frustration, disappointment, and pain. Forgiveness was at the cross, love was at the cross, repentance was at the cross, compassion was at the cross, and insurmountable strength.

Pray and Faint Not

Jesus enables saints to be revived from fainting and He has supplied us with everything that we need to prevail. The psalmist proclaims to "Wait on the LORD: Be of good courage, and he shall strengthen your heart; Wait, I say, on the LORD!" (Psalm 27:14 NKJV). Waiting does not mean to remain inactive without a specific goal or purpose to attain. God requires our active participation in the ministry to avoid idleness. "Wait" literally means to expect spiritual strength to come from God as we wait courageously. The psalmist warns us twice to "wait," do not proceed, *stand still,* and wait on the LORD with expectation. Waiting can be our worst enemy because we become impatient and proceed without caution. Are you willing to wait on God? Are you willing to wait for your healing? Are you willing to wait for your breakthrough? Are you willing to wait for your miracle? Do you believe your blessing is on the way? He is the ultimate source who revitalizes saints when all of their might is gone.

Physical exertion is never replenished with supplements like a "red bull drink" that increases your metabolic rate, literally hyping you up and later leaving you with after effects that are not beneficial for your health. Your body needs to be revitalized spiritually in order to function in its fullest capacity physically, spiritually, and intellectually. When God strengthens you, faintness dissipates and energy increases. Faintness is only temporary when you are a child of the King. He rejuvenates, replenishes, and restores your soul to overcome trials. Whenever we encounter bouts of faintness, we must remain prayerful and surround ourselves with men and women of God.

Jesus' atoning blood gives us the strength and satisfaction to prevail in any situation. If you expect an answer from God, you must pray fervently and sincerely with expectation and faith. Your life must align with the Word of God and His commandments, representing you as a beacon of light and an ambassador of Christ. "Let us then approach the throne of grace with confidence, so that we may receive mercy and find grace to help us in our time of need" (Hebrews 4:16). Prayers that display confidence in times of need illustrate to God our sincerity in receiving His mercy and grace. Coming to the throne of God boldly with holy hands lifted and a heart filled with reverence receives incredible blessings from God.

We need God's grace and mercy, particularly when we are experiencing spiritual warfare. His unmerited favor upon our lives acknowledges His love for us, and our continuous prayers connect us to a sovereign God. What a privilege it is to take our burdens to the Lord in prayer! We serve a God who is greater than any obstacle we may encounter in this world. He imparts hope to the hopeless, shows mercy to the merciless, and gives victory to the defeated. Who is willing to wrestle with the Lord like Jacob and declare, "Any way you bless me, I will be satisfied"? Hold on to God's unchanging hand!

Remember: "Do not be afraid or discouraged, for the LORD God, my God, is with you" (1 Chronicles 28:20). Continue to be vigilant in prayer, because your prayers are not in vain.

Jesus esteems prayer, and His directives are clear: "pray and do not faint." The undertaking of prayer develops confidence, which emphasizes the necessity to speak with God. Prayer abates idleness and builds spiritual maturity. Men should pray to abort faintness, pursue persistence, and embrace endurance. We draw from God's strength as He extracts our vulnerabilities and imputes wisdom. When we are mindful of God's plan, He is mindful of our future and we are the recipients' of God's blessings.

Jesus insists that we should never neglect prayer or devalue its merit. Prayer should take precedence in our lives, and heaven must be on our minds while we are on our knees. Jesus implied that men should not lose heart or become discouraged or bewildered. Therefore, exercise prayer wholeheartedly without revocation, because we receive the promises of God when we pray vigilantly, and refrain from collapsing.

Remember, fainting is a temporary situation revealed when we are disheartened, but faintness can be resolved. God is capable of replenishing our souls. Our obligation is to pray; God's responsibility is to respond. Men should make a conscientious effort to embrace prayer because the answers to our prayers do not reside within us, but rather within God. Be mindful that a prayer life without challenges is a prayer life without growth, but a consecrated prayer life is a spiritual life blessed by God. Prayer never fails especially during trials, because we serve a God without imperfections who possesses supernatural abilities' to prevail through any adversity.

Endnotes

[1] Thayer and Smith. "Greek Lexicon entry for *Proseuche*" Retrieved September 6, 2010, from *"The New Testament Greek Lexicon."* (http://www.studylight.org/lex/grk/view.cgi?number=3670).

[2] Harding, *Pronouncing Bible Dictionary*, 1873, p. 250.

[3] Thayer and Smith. "Greek Lexicon entry for *Homologeo.*" Retrieved September 6, 2010, from *"The New Testament Greek Lexicon."* (http://www.studylight.org/lex/grk/view.cgi?number=3670).

[4] Joy. (n.d.). *Collins English Dictionary - Complete & Unabridged 10th Edition.* Retrieved September 06, 2010, from Dictionary.com website: (http://dictionary.reference.com/browse/joy).

[5] Strength. (n.d.). *Dictionary.com Unabridged.* Retrieved September 07, 2010, from Dictionary.com website: (http://dictionary.reference.com/browse/strength).

[6] Avail. (n.d.). *The American Heritage® Dictionary of Idioms* by Christine Ammer. Retrieved June 03, 2009, from Dictionary.com website: (http://dictionary.classic.reference.com/browse/avail).

[7] Effectual. (n.d.). *The American Heritage® Dictionary of the English Language, Fourth Edition.* Retrieved May 05, 2008, from Dictionary.com website: (http://dictionary.reference.com/browse/effectual).

[8] Fervent. (n.d.). *Dictionary.com Unabridged.* Retrieved September 07, 2010, from Dictionary.com website: (http://dictionary.reference.com/browse/fervent).

[9] Shekinah. (n.d.). *Dictionary.com Unabridged (v 1.1).* Retrieved August 10, 2009, from Dictionary.com website: (http://dictionary.reference.com/browse/shekinah).

[10] Intercession. James Strong, L.L.D., S.T.D. *The New Strong's Exhaustive Concordance of Bible.* Nashville, Tennessee: Thomas Nelson Publishers, 1995, p. 112.

[11] Strife. (n.d.). *Dictionary.com Unabridged (v 1.1).* Retrieved September 12, 2009, from Dictionary.com (http://dictionary.reference.com/browse/strife).

[12] Brown, Driver, Briggs, and Gesenius. "Hebrew Lexicon entry for Ya`aph". Retrieved September 7, 2010, from, "The KJV Old Testament Hebrew Lexicon." (http://www.searchgodsword.org/lex/heb/view.cgi?number=3286).

[13] Thayer and Smith. "Greek Lexicon entry for Thlipsis." Retrieved September 7, 2010 from, "The New Testament Greek Lexicon." (http://www.studylight.org/lex/grk/view.cgi?number=2347).

Berney K. Dorton

Breinigsville, PA USA
30 March 2011
258717BV00002B/1/P